CREATIVE COOKING FOR TWO

Edited by
Jane Solmson

WEATHERVANE
BOOKS

contents

introduction

American tradition is bound by family gatherings, many revolving around mealtime. Most of us remember all-day preparations of luscious dishes serving eight, ten, or even twenty on special occasions. All too often these memorable meals are lost when children grow up and families scatter.

Creative Cooking for Two brings back the excitement and variety of the mouth-watering dishes you remember so well, with recipes just right for two. Cooking for two people used to be plain and unimaginative. Now it can be an adventure.

College roommates and working couples will love the quickness with which full meals can be prepared. Inexperienced cooks will be amazed at the easy-to-understand instructions that allow them to cook the most elaborate dishes without wasteful leftovers. Everyone will appreciate the fantastic tastes and aromas created by the dozens of wonderful recipes found on the following pages.

Renew interest in breakfast with combinations of eggs, fruits, grains, and yogurts. Spice up lunches with soups for two and fluffy omelets filled with everything from mushrooms to coconut. Prepare elegant dinners with chicken or duck, fish or lobster, pork or filet mignon in delicate sauces to enhance flavor.

Yes, Americans thrive on hearty, rib-sticking meals. But your working and living habits don't always allow you to dine with all your loved ones at the same time. Now this super cookbook allows you to create those wonderful, home-cooked meals every night for you and your guest. When family and friends join you, just double or triple these recipes to accommodate the appetites of everyone.

breakfast

Nutritionists agree that breakfast is one of the most important meals of the day. Offered here are suggestions from Quick Breakfast-In-A-Glass when time is an item to a relaxed Alpine Breakfast for more leisurely days.

alpine breakfast

1 banana, sliced
2 tablespoons lemon juice
1 slice canned pineapple
½ cup red currants, raspberries, or
    blueberries
⅔ to 1 cup rolled oats
1 cup plain or fruit-flavored yogurt
¼ cup cottage cheese
2 tablespoons rum or drop of rum
    flavoring
¼ teaspoon ground ginger
2 tablespoons honey

Sprinkle banana with lemon juice.

Cut pineapple into small pieces; set aside few pieces for use as garnish.

Mix banana, pineapple, and berries with oats; spoon into 2 bowls.

Blend together yogurt, cottage cheese, rum, ginger, and honey. Pour over cereal; garnish with reserved pineapple.

alpine breakfast

instant breakfast

1 cup cold milk
1 egg
3 tablespoons undiluted orange-juice concentrate

Blend all ingredients in blender at high speed until frothy. Serve immediately.

quick breakfast-in-a-glass

For a breakfast-on-the-run.

2 cups plain yogurt
2 eggs
⅓ cup wheat germ
⅓ cup frozen orange-juice
    concentrate
¼ cup honey or light molasses

Combine all ingredients in blender; blend until smooth. Serve at once.

buttermilk pancakes

⁷/₈ cup flour
1 teaspoon sugar
½ teaspoon baking soda
¾ teaspoon baking powder
1 cup sour milk*
2 tablespoons butter
1 egg

buttermilk pancakes

Mix flour, sugar, soda, and baking powder. Add ½ cup milk; mix very gently.
Melt butter. Let cool.
Mix egg with butter, using fork. Add remaining milk; mix very thoroughly.
Add slowly to flour batter, mixing very gently and as little as possible. (There will
be lumps.) Fry in lightly greased skillet, flipping to fry both sides.

*Regular milk can be made sour by adding 2 tablespoons lemon juice.

green-banana porridge

3 green bananas
1 tablespoon cold water
¼ cup milk
Sugar and salt
1 tablespoon flour
2 tablespoons coconut cream

Grate bananas. Stir in water and milk; beat well until smooth. Add salt; cook 1 hour, stirring. Add flour to thicken if necessary. Add coconut cream 10 minutes before serving.

eggs

Cooking with eggs adds high protein value to the diet combined with delicious different taste treats. Use the recipes offered here as breakfast variations or for light and pleasing suppers.

scrambled eggs

4 eggs
¼ cup milk
½ teaspoon Tabasco

1 teaspoon salt
3 tablespoons butter

Mix all ingredients, except butter, in bowl. Vigorously whip together until consistent and starting to foam.

Heat butter to very hot. Add egg mixture. Scrape across bottom as eggs coagulate. Serve medium rare.

scrambled eggs japanese

4 fresh mushrooms, sliced
2 scallions, cut into ½-inch pieces
Butter or oil

4 eggs, lightly beaten
Few sprinkles of soy sauce
½ teaspoon sherry (optional)

Slice mushrooms and scallions; sauté in butter 2 minutes.

Beat eggs. Add soy sauce and sherry; scramble in skillet with mushrooms and scallions until sufficiently cooked.

eggs, zucchini, and lox

A meal in a frying pan.

3 tablespoons vegetable oil
1 onion, minced
1 large stalk celery, sliced
1 clove garlic, minced
1 pound zucchini, washed, unpared,
    coarsely grated

1 carrot, coarsely grated
Salt and pepper
Lemon juice
4 slices lox, cut into small pieces
2 eggs, beaten

Heat oil in 10-inch skillet. Cook onion, celery, and garlic clove until soft. Add zucchini and carrot. Cook over low heat uncovered, about 10 minutes, stirring occasionally. Season with salt, pepper, and lemon juice to taste. Add lox; cook few minutes. Pour eggs over zucchini mix; cook few minutes longer, until egg is set.

eggs in snow

eggs in snow

An innovative variation of the simplest of all snacks—eggs on toast.

2 slices bread
Butter
2 eggs
Salt and pepper
Nutmeg
Grated cheese

Toast bread lightly. Butter; keep hot.

Separate eggs. Add salt, pepper, and nutmeg to egg whites; beat until stiff. Spread egg white over buttered toast. Make slight indentation in middle of each slice; drop an egg yolk in each. Sprinkle with grated cheese. Put under hot broiler for few minutes, until egg yolks have set.

11

egg pouches

2 tablespoons butter
3 eggs, well beaten
½ tomato, chopped
2 green onions, chopped
½ cup crumbled feta cheese
½ teaspoon salt
⅛ teaspoon pepper
2 pieces pita bread

Melt butter in small, heavy skillet.

Combine eggs, vegetables, cheese, salt, and pepper. Pour into skillet; cook over low heat as you would scrambled eggs, until set.

Meanwhile, cut pockets in bread with sharp knife. If bread is large, cut in half; gently separate inside layers, being careful not to split open sides. For smaller bread, cut thin slice from top edge of bread; separate inside layers with sharp knife. Fill bread with egg mixture.

Serve egg pouches with mayonnaise.

spanish eggs with vegetables

Diced ham can be substituted for chorizo sausage.

1 small onion or shallot, finely
    chopped
1 tablespoon butter
1 medium cooked potato, diced
1 clove garlic, pressed
2 medium tomatoes, skinned
1 red sweet pepper, chopped
½ cup chopped chorizo sausage
Salt and pepper to taste
2 eggs

Sauté onion in butter in small, heavy skillet until tender. Stir in potato, garlic, tomatoes, sweet pepper, and sausage. Cook over medium heat, stirring constantly, until heated through. Add salt and pepper. Turn potato mixture into 2 small oven-proof bowls; make indentation in center of each. Place an egg in each indentation; cover bowls lightly with foil. Bake in preheated 350°F oven 10 minutes or until eggs are set but not hard.

Serve garnished with chopped parsley or chives if desired.

spanish eggs with vegetables

13

artichoke omelet

4 tablespoons olive oil
1 clove garlic, minced
2 green onions, chopped
2 teaspoons chopped parsley
1 8½-ounce can artichoke hearts, cut
    in half
4 eggs, well-beaten

Heat oil in medium-size skillet or 9-inch omelet pan. Add garlic and green onions; sauté 1 minute. Add parsley and artichoke hearts; sauté 3 minutes. Add eggs. Lower heat; cook until eggs are set.

Serve omelet with tomato sauce.

bacon and potato omelet

3 slices bacon, cut into small pieces
2 small potatoes, peeled, sliced
8 fresh spinach leaves, stems
    removed, sliced into ¼-inch
    slices
6 eggs, lightly beaten with fork
½ cup yogurt
Salt and pepper to taste

Heat bacon briefly in 10-inch skillet. Add potatoes; fry until bacon is crisp and potatoes are lightly browned. Add spinach; remove mixture to small bowl.

Combine eggs, yogurt, salt, and pepper. Pour into skillet. Distribute potato mixture evenly over them. Cook over low heat without stirring. As eggs set on bottom, lift edges; allow uncooked mixture to run underneath. When omelet is set, fold with fork. Serve immediately.

Picture on opposite page: bacon and potato omelet

14

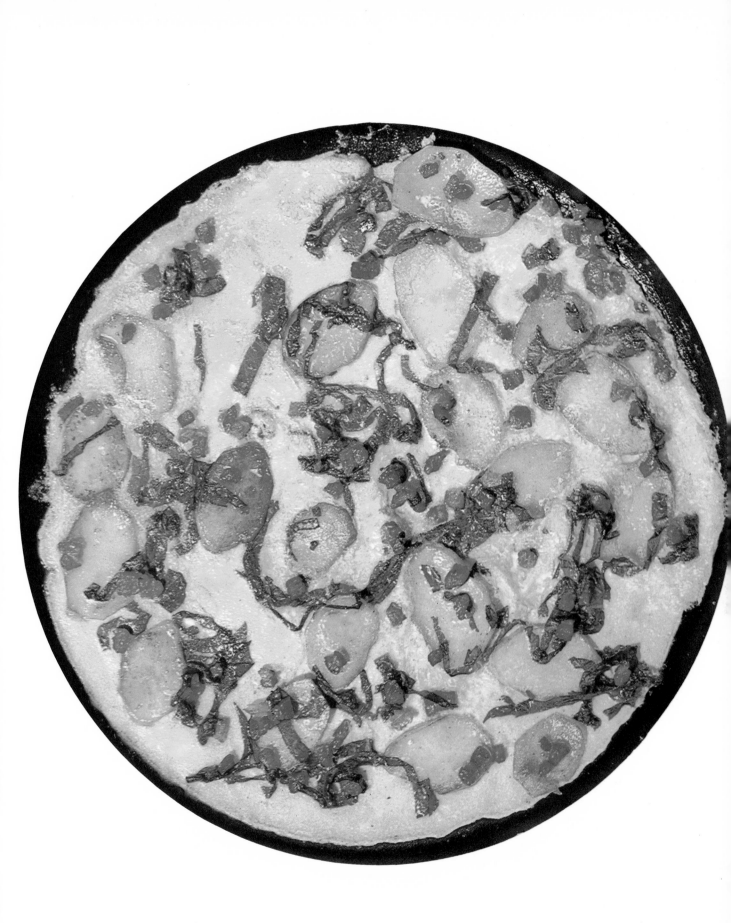

puffy omelet

¼ cup water
¼ teaspoon salt
¼ teaspoon cream of tartar
4 eggs, separated
1 tablespoon butter

Add water, salt, and cream of tartar to egg whites; beat until stiff but not dry, or just until whites no longer slip when bowl is tilted.

Beat egg yolks until thick and lemon-colored, about 5 minutes. Fold yolks into whites. On medium-high heat heat butter in omelet pan or 10-inch skillet with oven-proof handle until just hot enough to sizzle a drop of water. Pour in omelet mixture; gently smooth surface. Reduce heat to medium; cook slowly until puffy and lightly browned on bottom, about 5 minutes. Lift omelet at edge to judge color. Bake in preheated 350°F oven 10 to 12 minutes or until knife inserted halfway between center and outside edge comes out clean.

To serve, loosen omelet edges with spatula. With sharp knife cut upper surface down center of omelet, but *do not* cut through to bottom of omelet. Fill, if desired. Tip skillet; with pancake turner, fold omelet in half. Turn out onto platter with quick flip of the wrist. Serve immediately.

omelet with tomato–green pepper sauce

tomato–green pepper sauce

2 tablespoons olive oil
1 green pepper, cut into slices

1 clove garlic, minced
1 8-ounce can tomato sauce

Make sauce first. Heat oil in small saucepan or skillet. Add pepper and garlic; sauté 3 minutes. Add tomato sauce. Lower heat to simmer. Simmer 15 minutes.

omelet

4 eggs, well beaten
1 tablespoon water
Salt and pepper

2 tablespoons butter
½ cup crumbled feta cheese

Beat eggs with water. Add salt and pepper to taste.

In 8-inch omelet pan or small skillet heat butter over medium heat until it sizzles. Add egg mixture; reduce heat to low. As eggs begin to set, carefully lift edges of omelet with spatula; let uncooked eggs flow to bottom of pan. When omelet is almost done, sprinkle with feta cheese. Fold omelet.

Serve omelet topped with Tomato–Green Pepper Sauce.

bread omelet

Serve this hearty dish with grilled meats or as a substitute for potatoes. It can also be served as a main dish for supper.

3 eggs
Salt and pepper to taste
1½ teaspoons finely chopped fresh
    parsley

1 tablespoon butter
½ cup Fried Croutons
2 tablespoons grated Parmesan
    cheese

Beat eggs lightly with fork. Season with salt and pepper. Add parsley; beat again.

Melt butter in 9-inch omelet pan until butter just begins to brown around edge. Add egg mixture; reduce heat. Lift around edge with fork or spatula; tilt pan to allow egg to run underneath. Cook until browned and set on bottom but top is still moist. Sprinkle croutons to within 1 inch of edge; sprinkle with 1 tablespoon cheese. Flip over; slide onto heated plate.

Sprinkle omelet with remaining cheese. Serve immediately.

fried croutons

Dried slices day-old bread   Butter

For small croutons, cut crusts from bread; cut slices into about ½-inch squares.

Melt ¼ cup butter for each 2 cups bread squares in heavy saucepan or skillet. Toss bread in butter to coat evenly, using pancake turner. Fry over medium heat until croutons are golden, tossing continuously. Turn out onto paper toweling to drain and cool.

Use croutons in salads or soups. Can be stored in airtight container several days.

bread omelet

mushroom omelet

mushroom topping

   1 cup sliced fresh mushrooms
   2 tablespoons butter or margarine
   ½ cup plain yogurt
   ½ teaspoon dillweed

Sauté mushrooms in butter in 10-inch skillet or omelet pan until tender, about 2 or 3 minutes. Remove from pan. Cool to room temperature; add yogurt and dill.

omelet

   1 tablespoon butter or margarine
   4 eggs
   ½ teaspoon salt

Melt butter in skillet or omelet pan.

Lightly mix eggs and salt with fork; pour into skillet. As edges set, lift gently to allow uncooked portions to run underneath. When omelet is cooked through but still moist, top with mushroom mixture. Carefully roll omelet out of pan onto warm platter.

ambrosia omelet

Nice for a ladies' luncheon or a summer brunch.

fruit topping

   ½ cup yogurt
   2 teaspoons sugar
   ½ cup sliced strawberries

   ½ cup drained pineapple tidbits
   ½ banana, sliced
   ¼ cup flaked coconut, toasted

Combine ingredients; set aside.

omelet

   1 tablespoon butter or margarine
   4 eggs

   ¼ teaspoon salt
   ¼ teaspoon grated lemon peel

Melt butter in 10-inch skillet or omelet pan.

Lightly mix eggs, salt, and lemon peel with fork; pour into skillet. As egg mixture sets, lift edges to allow uncooked portions to run underneath. When omelet is cooked through but still moist, top with fruit mixture.

Gently roll omelet out of pan onto warm platter. Serve at once.

chicken-liver omelet

liver filling

3 tablespoons butter	¾ cup chicken stock
2 tablespoons minced onion	1 teaspoon tomato paste
¼ cup chopped mushrooms	Salt and pepper
¼ pound chicken livers	⅛ teaspoon thyme
1 tablespoon flour	

Heat butter in skillet. Sauté onion, mushrooms, and livers until livers are browned. Remove from pan; keep hot.

Add flour to skillet; mix with pan juices. Add stock; stir until boiling. Add tomato paste, seasoning, and thyme; cook 5 minutes. Return livers to pan; reheat.

omelet

4 eggs	2 tablespoons cold water
¼ teaspoon salt	1 tablespoon butter
⅛ teaspoon black pepper	

Prepare omelet in usual way. Spread with liver mixture just before serving. Garnish with additional chicken livers.

19

cheese omelets

4 eggs, separated
White pepper to taste
½ cup freshly grated Parmesan
      cheese
Salt to taste
Butter

Beat egg yolks until thick and lemon-colored. Stir in pepper and cheese. Season with very small amount of salt; Parmesan cheese imparts salty flavor.

Beat egg whites in large bowl until stiff peaks form. Push egg whites to one side of bowl; turn cheese mixture into bowl next to egg whites. Fold and cut cheese mixture into egg whites with rubber spatula until well blended.

Melt small amount butter on griddle over medium-high heat. Spoon half the cheese mixture onto hot griddle to form oblong loaf; repeat with remaining cheese mixture. Reduce heat to medium low. Shape omelets into neat ovals with table knife; cook until bottoms are lightly browned and set. Turn omelets with spatula; cook until lightly browned and set. Drizzle with melted butter.

appetizers/first course

Canapes or the all important first course for that special candle-lit meal for two make any meal a party. The appetizers included here are attractive in appearance and taste so good that you're sure to want more.

tomato fondue with cocktail frankfurters

Serve French bread separately and use small frankfurters for dipping.

1 clove garlic
2 cups grated cheddar or American
    cheese
½ cup grated Gruyère cheese
½ cup condensed tomato soup
1 teaspoon Worcestershire sauce
3 tablespoons dry sherry
1 small can cocktail frankfurters
French bread

Rub inside of fondue pot with cut garlic clove. Put in cheeses, tomato soup, and Worcestershire sauce; stir continuously over low heat until cheese has melted and mixture is creamy. Stir in sherry; cook 2 to 3 minutes. Adjust seasoning before serving.

Frankfurters are speared onto fondue forks and dipped into fondue. Serve with plenty of French bread.

clams casino

Worcestershire sauce
Hot pepper sauce
2 tablespoons cocktail sauce
Garlic powder to taste
Salt and pepper to taste
1 8-ounce can minced clams,
    partially drained
8 small empty clam shells
Italian bread crumbs
Pinch of parsley flakes
Bacon
Lemon wedges

Mix all sauces and seasonings with clams, allowing 2 drops Worcestershire and 2 drops hot pepper sauce per shell. Put some into each shell. Sprinkle bread crumbs lightly over each shell. Follow with pinch of parsley flakes over each. Cover each filled shell with piece of raw bacon. Arrange shells in oven until bacon is done. Arrange 4 shells on plate. Serve with lemon wedges.

Can be served with steamed shrimp on the same dish.

tomato fondue with cocktail frankfurters

egg foo yong

3 eggs, beaten
1 teaspoon soy sauce
1 teaspoon dry sherry
¾ cup drained canned Chinese
    vegetables (half of 16-ounce can)
About ½ cup meat shreds, canned
    shrimp, or chicken
1 2-ounce can sliced mushrooms,
    drained
2 tablespoons butter or margarine
2 tablespoons cooking oil
1 8-ounce can peas, drained

Mix eggs, soy sauce, sherry, vegetables, and meat. Add mushrooms; save few pieces for topping. Mix and spoon 4 patties into hot butter and oil in large skillet, using half the mixture. Fry until brown on both sides. Remove to heated plate; keep in warm oven while remaining 4 patties are being fried. Arrange last patties on second plate; place in oven while sauce is prepared and peas are heating.

Heat peas; drain.

Garnish plates with peas and reserved mushrooms. Pour sauce over all.

egg foo yong sauce

1 cup chicken broth (or 1 cup water
    with chicken bouillon cube
    dissolved in it)
1 teaspoon soy sauce
1 teaspoon dry sherry
2 teaspoons cornstarch

Combine broth, soy sauce, and sherry in small saucepan. Dissolve cornstarch in cup in small amount of mixture from the saucepan. Put back in pan; cook few minutes, until clear and slightly thickened.

grapefruit with crab

2 grapefruit
1 cup (8 ounces) crab meat
Little mayonnaise
Parsley or lemon slices for garnish

Mix flesh from grapefruit with crab meat. Bind with mayonnaise; season to taste.

Serve in grapefruit shells, garnished with parsley or lemon slices.

grapefruit with crab

25

soups

If you want to be more original than just opening a can, try Cold Yogurt Soup or Spinach Soup. Included in this section is a nice variety of unusual soups to start off that dinner-for-two with your own special touch.

blueberry soup

1½ cups fresh blueberries or dry-
    pack frozen blueberries, rinsed,
    drained
2 cups water
½ cup sugar
1 tablespoon lemon juice
1 cinnamon stick (2 inches)
¼ cup cornstarch
¼ cup water
½ cup heavy cream, whipped

Stir together blueberries, water, sugar, lemon juice, and cinnamon stick in medium saucepan. Bring to boil; reduce heat. Simmer, uncovered, 15 minutes.

Stir cornstarch and water until smooth. Add to blueberry mixture. Cook over medium heat, stirring constantly, until mixture comes to boil; boil 1 minute. Chill.

Serve soup garnished with dollop of whipped cream.

cold yogurt soup

3 cucumbers
Salt
1 clove garlic, cut
1 tablespoon vinegar
1 teaspoon dill
1 pint yogurt
Chopped mint

Peel cucumbers. Cut in quarters lengthwise; slice. Place in bowl; sprinkle with salt.

Rub another bowl with garlic. Swish vinegar in to collect flavor. Add dill and yogurt. Stir until thick. Pour over cucumbers.

Sprinkle soup with chopped mint. Serve cold.

curried pea soup

10-ounce package frozen green peas
½ cup water
1 chicken bouillon cube
½ cup diced onion
1 rib celery, diced
1 clove garlic, minced
½ teaspoon salt
½ teaspoon curry powder
White pepper to taste
1 cup milk
½ medium lemon

Bring peas, water, bouillon cube, onion, celery, garlic, salt, curry powder, and pepper to boil. Cover; simmer until vegetables are soft. Puree in electric blender. Add milk; whirl to blend. Heat, squeezing in lemon juice. If thicker than you like, add water or milk; correct seasoning.

potato soup

2 large potatoes, peeled, cubed
1 medium onion
¼ cup margarine
2 tablespoons flour
Salt and pepper to taste

Put potatoes into saucepan. Cover with water; simmer until fork-tender.

In separate pot sauté the onion in margarine until golden brown. Add flour; mix over low heat until smooth. Add small amount of water from potatoes; mix thoroughly. Add potatoes and remaining water; bring to boil, stirring constantly. Season to taste with salt and pepper.

Picture on opposite page: potato soup

spinach soup

⅓ cup spinach, cooked, chopped
10½-ounce can cream of chicken
    soup, condensed
1⅓ cups milk
Few grains salt
Few grains pepper
Croutons
Paprika

Mix ingredients, except croutons and paprika. Cook over moderate heat, stirring occasionally, until flavors are blended.

Serve soup garnished with croutons, paprika, or generous tablespoon of thick cream if desired.

Note: Chopped cooked broccoli can be used in place of spinach.

spinach soup

oyster bisque

2 tablespoons butter
2 tablespoons flour
1 pint milk
12 oysters (cut small)
1 cup oyster liquor
Celery, cut fine, cooked (optional)
Salt, pepper, and paprika

Blend butter with flour; add hot milk.

Heat oysters and liquor slowly; let come to boiling point. Add to milk mixture; season to taste with salt, pepper, and paprika. Add cooked celery if desired.

Serve soup very hot, with crackers.

sandwiches

Bread is indeed the staff of life and the basis for the all-American sandwich. But the filling can change the ordinary into something special. Have you ever tried a Strawberry Sandwich? Read on and then go out for fresh berries in season.

feta-cheese sandwiches

2 pita-bread rounds
8 ½-inch slices feta cheese
1 cup finely shredded lettuce
½ medium tomato, diced
¼ cup diced cucumber
2 tablespoons chopped green pepper
2 radishes, thinly sliced
3 tablespoons oil-and-vinegar salad
    dressing

Warm bread. Cut in half; form pocket in each half. Place 2 cheese slices in each pocket.

Combine vegetables and salad dressing in bowl. Stuff each bread pocket with some of salad mixture.

open-face sardine sandwiches

¼ cup mayonnaise
¼ cup commercial sour cream
Tabasco sauce to taste
1 small scallion, thinly sliced
2 English muffins, split
2 slices cheddar cheese
2 slices tomato
3¾-ounce can brisling
    sardines, drained
Paprika

Using fork, beat together mayonnaise, sour cream, and Tabasco to blend in small jar. Stir in scallion.

Lightly toast muffin halves; place well apart on sheet of foil. Put cheese slice on each half, making sure muffin edges are covered, so they won't scorch. Top cheese with tomato and sardines. Spoon mayonnaise mixture over sardines; sprinkle with paprika. Broil about 4 to 6 inches from high heat until cheese melts—sandwiches will be hot through.

strawberry sandwiches

Whole-wheat bread, toasted
2 ounces cream cheese
4 teaspoons orange marmalade
4 to 6 strawberries, sliced

Spread toast with cream cheese and thin layer of marmalade. Add layer of strawberries.

chicken club sandwich

Bread slices
Butter
Mayonnaise
Lettuce
Slices of chicken breast

Prepared mustard
8 slices bacon, fried crisp
2 to 4 slices tomato or onion
Gherkins or stuffed olives for garnish

Remove crusts from bread. Toast; spread with butter. Spread first slice with a little mayonnaise; cover with 1 or 2 lettuce leaves and slices of chicken. Spread a little more mayonnaise on chicken; cover with second slice of toast. Spread a very little mustard on toast, then a little mayonnaise. Cover with bacon and tomato or onion slices. Place third toast slice on top; press down firmly.

Serve sandwich at once, garnished with slices of gherkin or stuffed olive.

salads

Allow your salad to compliment any meal or use it as a main course. Include all kinds of fresh vegetables in season and don't forget vegetables in season and don't forget fresh fruit. Salads are appealing to the eye as well as the taste buds — and they're good for you, too.

avocado salad vinaigrette

1 recipe Vinaigrette
8 green onions or scallions
½ large red sweet pepper

2 avocados, peeled
Lemon juice
Watercress or chopped romaine

Prepare Vinaigrette.

Trim onions, leaving about 2 inches of green stems; cut into ½-inch lengths.

Remove seeds and white membrane from pepper; cut into thin lengthwise slices.

Cut avocados in half; remove seeds. Cut 1 avocado into lengthwise slices. Dip halves and slices into lemon juice to prevent discoloration.

Arrange watercress, pepper, onion, and avocados on serving dish as shown in illustration.

Shake Vinaigrette to blend. Fill avocado halves with sauce.

vinaigrette

2 teaspoons salt
½ teaspoon freshly ground pepper
1 teaspoon prepared mustard

1 cup olive oil
½ cup tarragon wine vinegar

Put salt, pepper, and mustard in medium-size bowl. Add several drops of olive oil; blend with wooden spoon. Add several drops of vinegar; blend well. Add remaining oil and vinegar gradually, stirring constantly, until all is used. Store in covered jar in refrigerator. Shake well before using.

avocado salad vinaigrette

beet salad

1 garlic clove, halved
Lettuce
1 medium-size can beets, diced
2 small onions, sliced
1 7-ounce can tuna
2 hard-boiled eggs, sliced
4 ounces mayonnaise
¼ teaspoon salt
Pepper

Rub salad bowl with garlic. Line bowl with lettuce leaves. Put beets, onions, tuna, and eggs in another bowl.

Combine mayonnaise, salt, and pepper. Toss gently with beet mixture. Serve in salad bowl.

crab-meat salad

1 can crab meat (5½ or 6 ounces)
1 small rib celery, finely minced
1 tablespoon chopped onion (or 1
    teaspoon dried onion flakes)
1 tablespoon dill-pickle relish
2 tablespoons mayonnaise
1 tablespoon plain yogurt
1 tablespoon lemon juice
1 hard-cooked egg, chopped
Salt or seasoned salt
Pepper
Paprika
Lettuce
Lemon wedges
Parsley

Combine crab, celery, onion, relish, mayonnaise, yogurt, lemon juice, and egg; toss lightly. Season to taste.

Arrange on beds of lettuce; garnish with lemon wedges and parsley.

quick-and-easy cucumber salad

1 large cucumber, sliced
2 scallions, sliced into 1-inch pieces

salad dressing

1½ teaspoons soy sauce
2½ tablespoons sugar
6 tablespoons vinegar

Slice cucumber (do not peel).
Slice scallions; toss with cucumber.
Mix together soy sauce, sugar, and vinegar. Adjust amounts to taste.
Pour dressing over vegetables; toss well. Sprinkle a few sesame seeds on top if desired.

grapefruit mold

1 envelope unflavored gelatin
2 tablespoons sugar
1½ cups grapefruit juice
2 tablespoons cream sherry or sherry flavoring
1 can (8 ounces) fruit cocktail, drained
Orange slices and halved strawberries for garnish

Mix gelatin, sugar, and ½ cup juice in small saucepan. Stir over low heat until gelatin is completely dissolved. Stir in remaining juice and sherry. Chill until mixture becomes syrupy.
Fold in fruit cocktail. Pour mixture into 1-pint mold; chill until firm.
To unmold, dip mold into lukewarm water, tap to loosen, and invert onto platter. Chill until ready to serve. Garnish with orange slices and strawberry halves.

38

greek-goddess salad

1 eggplant
Lemon juice
1 teaspoon salt
1 teaspoon oregano
¼ teaspoon garlic salt
½ cup olive oil
2 cups diced cooked lamb
1 cup minced parsley
1 cup chopped celery
¼ cup sliced green onion
2 tomatoes, sliced
1 tablespoon sugar
1 tablespoon lemon juice
2 tablespoons vinegar
1 teaspoon mint
¹/₈ teaspoon pepper

Cut eggplant in half lengthwise. Scoop out pulp; dice. Brush inside of shells with lemon juice.

Cook and stir diced eggplant, salt, oregano, and garlic salt in hot oil until tender. Remove to large bowl. Add lamb, parsley, celery, green onion, and tomatoes.

Mix sugar, 1 tablespoon lemon juice, vinegar, mint, and pepper. Pour over eggplant mixture. Cover; chill 2 hours. Fill eggplant shells to serve.

spinach salad

3 ounces olive oil
2 ounces red-wine vinegar
1 ounce red wine
1 teaspoon Worcestershire sauce
1 teaspoon prepared mustard
1 teaspoon sugar
½ package fresh spinach, washed,
   dried
4 slices crisp crumbled bacon
1 hard-boiled egg, crumbled
⅓ red onion, diced

Heat together oil, vinegar, and wine. Add Worcestershire sauce, mustard, and sugar. Pour over spinach. Sprinkle bacon, egg, and onion over salad. Serve at room temperature.

grapefruit salad

Sunshine-yellow grapefruit salad and cool green cucumber slices make this a very appetizing presentation.

2 firm grapefruit
1 cup diced cold cooked potatoes
½ cup diced unpeeled cucumber
Juice of 1 small orange, strained
2 tablespoons mayonnaise
1 tablespoon sour cream
2 teaspoons lemon juice
⅛ teaspoon paprika

Cut small slice from stem end of grapefruit, to prevent tipping. Slice off ⅓ of tops of grapefruit; reserve tops. Cut edges of grapefruit Vandyke fashion with kitchen shears or small sharp knife. Remove grapefruit sections carefully, using small sharp knife and fingers. Remove excess pith from shells and all pith and membrane from grapefruit sections. Drain sections thoroughly.

Combine grapefruit sections, potatoes, and cucumber in medium bowl.

Boil orange juice in small pan until reduced to 1 teaspoon liquid; let cool.

Add mayonnaise, sour cream, lemon juice, paprika, and orange juice to grapefruit mixture; toss lightly. Chill thoroughly.

Spoon grapefruit mixture into shells. Garnish tops of grapefruit with decorative leaves or parsley. Attach with toothpicks at slight angle over salad-filled shells.

tuna salad

1 7-ounce can flaked tuna
1 cup diced celery (or 1 teaspoon
        celery salt)
1 teaspoon minced onion
¼ cup fresh dressing
1 large cucumber
Salt and pepper
Hard-boiled eggs (optional)

Combine tuna, celery, and onion. Toss with dressing.

Cut cucumber into very thin slices. Line bowl with cucumber slices. Fill with tuna mixture. Garnish with cucumber. Add hard-boiled eggs if desired.

grapefruit salad

orange and onion salad

tomato and herb salad

orange and onion salad

3 oranges
1 Spanish onion
2 tablespoons tarragon or
    white-wine vinegar
4 tablespoons salad oil

Salt and black pepper
Pinch of paprika
Pinch of sugar
Chopped parsley

Peel oranges, removing all white pith; cut into thin slices.

Peel onion; slice thinly. Separate slices into rings. Arrange orange and onion slices alternately in serving dish.

Combine vinegar and oil; add salt, black pepper, paprika, and sugar; shake well. Pour over orange and onion. Marinate at least 1 hour.

Sprinkle salad with chopped parsley before serving.

stuffed pineapple

1 fresh pineapple

ham stuffing

8 ounces cooked ham, cubed
6 ounces sauerkraut
1 medium apple
Pineapple pieces

salad dressing

3 tablespoons mayonnaise
2 tablespoons heavy cream
Juice of 1 lemon
1 teaspoon fresh chopped dill or ¼
    teaspoon dried dill
¼ teaspoon rosemary
¼ teaspoon sugar
Salt (optional)

stuffed pineapple

Cut pineapple in half lengthwise. Scoop out; cut pineapple into bite-size pieces.
Rinse and drain sauerkraut.
Core unpeeled apple; cut into thin slices.
Gently mix above ingredients. Fill 2 pineapple halves with stuffing.
Thoroughly blend dressing ingredients. Pour dressing over salad. Let marinate
and chill in refrigerator 30 minutes.

tomato and herb salad

This salad is very easy to prepare. Good served with almost any barbecued
meat or fish.

Firm tomatoes
Salt
Olive oil
Wine vinegar or lemon juice
Chopped herbs (parsley, chives, dill,
    basil, tarragon, etc.)

Peel tomatoes; cut into fairly thick slices. Arrange on platter. Sprinkle with a
little salt, few drops olive oil, and wine vinegar or lemon juice. Sprinkle thickly with
chopped herbs. Chill before serving.

fruit salad

1 cup diced pineapple
1 cup diced papaya
¼ cup diced oranges
1 tablespoon lemon juice
1½ tablespoons sugar
½ cup coconut milk

Assemble fruit in bowl.
Add lemon juice and sugar to coconut milk; stir. Pour over fruit.

pasta

Don't be fooled into the idea that pasta is only for a large crowd. Two will enjoy ample portions of pasta without the problem of unwanted leftovers. There are as many varieties of pasta as there are cooks. Start with the recipes here and then try to create some of your own.

spaghetti with génoise sauce

1½ tablespoons salad oil
1 7-ounce package spaghetti
1 recipe Génoise Sauce

Bring 6 cups heavily salted water to boil. Add salad oil. Add spaghetti slowly; cook about 12 minutes or to desired doneness. Drain well; place in serving dish. Add sauce; toss gently.

génoise sauce

2 tablespoons finely chopped basil
    leaves
2 cloves garlic, pressed
½ teaspoon salt
½ cup freshly grated Parmesan
    cheese
½ cup olive oil

Place basil, garlic, and salt in wooden bowl; pound with pestle, or press to paste with back of wooden spoon. Work in cheese. Add oil, a drop at a time, until well combined.

spaghetti caruso

½ pound chicken livers
½ teaspoon salt
2 tablespoons butter
2 cups fresh sliced mushrooms
1 tablespoon instant minced onion or
    ¼ cup chopped raw onion
½ teaspoon mixed Italian herbs
1 8-ounce can tomato sauce
Hot cooked spaghetti

Sprinkle livers with salt. Brown in hot butter; remove from skillet.
Add mushrooms to skillet; sauté 5 minutes. (If raw onions are used, sauté now also.) Return livers to skillet; add instant onion, herbs, and tomato sauce. Simmer 3 to 5 minutes or until livers are done. (Do not overcook.) Serve over hot spaghetti.

garlic sauce for spaghetti

¼ cup oil
2 or 3 mashed garlic cloves

Heat oil with garlic. Pour oil over cooked spaghetti; toss.
For variations, add 1 teaspoon oregano or 1 tablespoon chopped parsley or ½ cup cooked clams just before removing oil from pan.

baked grits

1¼ cups milk
¼ teaspoon salt
Few grains pepper
1 tablespoon butter or margarine
¼ cup grits

Heat milk. Add seasonings and butter. Gradually stir in grits; cook until thickened, stirring constantly. Remove grits from heat; beat well. Place mixture in small greased casserole. Bake at 325°F until lightly browned, about 45 minutes.

chicken-noodle supper

1 8-ounce package egg noodles
1 can cream of chicken soup
2 5-ounce cans boned chicken
Salt and pepper

Cook noodles according to package directions. Combine with remaining ingredients. Heat 10 minutes.

pizza

crust

1½ cups all-purpose flour
½ teaspoon salt
1 package active dry yeast

½ cup warm water (105 to 115°F)
1 tablespoon vegetable oil

sauce

1 tablespoon olive oil
¼ cup finely chopped onion
1 clove garlic, minced
1 16-ounce can Italian-style peeled
　tomatoes

2 tablespoons tomato paste
½ teaspoon crumbled dried oregano
½ teaspoon sugar
½ teaspoon salt

topping

½ pound bulk sausage
1 cup shredded mozzarella cheese
¼ cup grated Parmesan cheese

1 4-ounce can sliced mushrooms,
　drained

Make the crust. Combine flour and salt; set aside. Dissolve yeast in warm water. Add oil. Stir in flour and salt. Turn out onto lightly floured board; knead until smooth and elastic. Lightly grease medium bowl. Place dough in bowl; rotate to grease whole surface. Cover bowl; put in warm place until double in bulk (1 to 1½ hours).

Meanwhile make sauce. Heat oil in medium saucepan. Add onion and garlic; sauté over medium heat 5 minutes, stirring constantly. Do not brown. Puree tomatoes and their juice in electric blender, or break up with fork. Add tomatoes, tomato paste, and seasonings to saucepan. Bring mixture to boil; reduce heat to low. Cook, uncovered, stirring occasionally, 50 minutes or until thick. Set aside to cool.

When the dough has doubled in bulk, punch down. Place dough on lightly floured surface; let rest 10 minutes. Roll to 12-inch circle; place in 12-inch-round pizza pan. Preheat oven to 400°F. Bake crust 13 to 15 minutes.

Meanwhile lightly fry sausage.

Remove crust from oven; top with sauce. Sprinkle with cheeses. Top with sausage and mushrooms. Return to oven; bake 10 minutes. Remove from pan; cut.

Note: The sauce recipe can be easily doubled and frozen for later use.

pizza

risotto

⁵⁄₈ cup long-grain rice
1 small onion
¼ cup butter
2½ cups vegetable stock or water
Salt and pepper
2 tablespoons grated Parmesan
    cheese

Wash and dry rice thoroughly.
Chop onion finely.
Heat butter. Fry onion until lightly browned. Add rice; fry until brown. Put in stock or water. Add salt and pepper to taste. Boil rapidly 10 minutes; simmer slowly until rice has absorbed all liquid. Stir in cheese. Add more seasoning if necessary. Garnish with mushroom cap if desired.

risotto

vegetables

Nutritious vegetables should be appetizing as well — and they are, when you prepare them in new and unusual ways. Enjoy new ideas in vegetables from asparagus to zucchini and you won't have to urge anyone to "finish your vegetables."

fresh asparagus

12 asparagus stalks
½ cup boiling water
½ teaspoon salt
Melted butter
Lemon juice

Cut away fibrous part of asparagus stalks. Tie together; place in tall pot. Add boiling water and salt. Cover; cook over medium heat about 8 minutes. Do not overcook. Drain. Pour over asparagus melted butter to which a little lemon juice has been added.

asparagus milanese

1 10-ounce package frozen asparagus
    spears, partially thawed
1 tablespoon melted butter or
    margarine, divided
2 tablespoons dry sherry
½ teaspoon seasoned salt and pepper
    mixture
⅓ cup Italian-style bread crumbs
2 tablespoons grated Romano cheese

Preheat oven to 350°F.
Separate asparagus spears; place in 9-inch pie plate.
Mix butter, sherry, and salt and pepper mixture; pour over asparagus. Tightly cover with foil; bake 30 minutes or until crisp-tender. Uncover; drain liquid from asparagus.
Melt remaining butter; combine with crumbs. Sprinkle over asparagus. Sprinkle with cheese. Broil until crumbs are lightly browned and cheese is melted.

Picture on next page: fresh asparagus

51

fresh green beans

fresh green beans

½ pound fresh green beans
Small amount water

Salt
Butter

Cook beans in water in tightly covered pan about 8 minutes or until just tender. Season with salt and butter before serving.

green beans italian

6 tablespoons chicken stock
2 tablespoons oil
4 peeled tomatoes, diced
1 pound string beans

Pinch of dried herbs
Salt and pepper
Chopped parsley

Combine stock, oil, and tomatoes; bring to boil. Add beans and herbs. Cover; simmer until beans are almost tender. Remove lid; simmer until excess liquid has evaporated. Add salt and pepper. Sprinkle with parsley.

fresh green beans with cherry tomatoes

Fresh green beans are accented with bright red cherry tomatoes. Use only fresh vegetables when preparing this dish.

½ **pound fresh green beans**
¾ **teaspoon salt**
1½ **tablespoons butter**
¼ **teaspoon sugar**
Dash of freshly ground pepper
2 teaspoons chopped fresh parsley
4 cherry tomatoes, halved

Wash beans; remove tips. Cut into 1-inch pieces. Place in saucepan with small amount boiling water and ½ teaspoon salt. Cook 5 minutes. Cover; cook over medium heat 10 to 15 minutes or until just crisp-tender. Drain if necessary. Add butter, sugar, pepper, remaining salt, and parsley. Toss lightly until butter is melted and beans are coated.

Place beans in serving bowl. Garnish with cherry tomatoes.

fresh green beans with cherry tomatoes

sweet-and-sour green beans

1 slice bacon, diced
½ teaspoon chopped onion
1 tablespoon vinegar

1 tablespoon water
¼ teaspoon sugar
8-ounce can green beans

Fry bacon until crisp; drain off excess fat. Add onion; cook until clear but not brown. Add remaining ingredients; mix lightly. Cook 5 minutes to heat beans.

frying-pan bean sprouts

2 cups fresh bean sprouts
Oil for frying, enough to cover bottom of pan
Sprinkles of soy sauce

Blanch sprouts in colander; rinse with cold water. Drain well.
Heat oil in frying pan until hot. Place sprouts in pan; toss until heated through. Cook quickly on high heat. Remove sprouts to serving plate. Sprinkle with soy sauce to taste.
If desired, chopped scallion can be added when cooking.

beets in orange sauce

orange sauce

1 tablespoon sugar
Few grains salt
1 teaspoon cornstarch

¼ cup orange juice
2 teaspoons lemon juice
1 teaspoon butter or margarine

Combine sugar, salt, and cornstarch; mix well. Stir in orange juice; cook and stir until thickened. Remove from heat. Blend in lemon juice and butter.

¾ cup or 8-ounce can beets, cooked or canned, sliced or diced

Add beets to Orange Sauce; reheat.

carrot pennies

1 cup sliced carrots (2 medium-size)
¼ cup water
1 teaspoon butter or margarine
1 teaspoon brown sugar

1 teaspoon water
Few grains salt
1½ teaspoons brandy or bourbon
   (optional)

Cook carrots in ¼ cup water until tender, about 10 minutes. Add remaining ingredients; mix lightly. Cook 3 minutes to blend flavors.

corn on the cob

2 to 4 husked ears of corn
Boiling water

Pinch of sugar
Soy sauce

Plunge corn into boiling water. Add pinch of sugar. Boil 10 to 15 minutes. Serve corn hot. Brush with soy sauce instead of butter.
Corn can be grilled instead of boiled.

corn on the cob

corn pudding

1 cup creamed corn
1 teaspoon salt
2 tablespoons melted butter
¼ cup bread crumbs

1 teaspoon flour
2 eggs
1 tablespoon flour

Mix all ingredients together. Bake at 350°F about 25 minutes, until pudding is firm.

breaded fried eggplant sticks

1 eggplant, peeled
1 egg, beaten
½ cup flour
¼ cup cornstarch

1 teaspoon salt
½ teaspoon pepper
Oil for frying

Cut eggplant into sticks about ¾ inch thick and 3 to 4 inches long. Dip in egg.
Mix together flour, cornstarch, salt, and pepper. Roll eggplant in mixture to coat.
Heat about 1 inch oil in skillet. Fry eggplant until golden, turning often. Remove; drain on absorbent paper.
Serve eggplant sticks with catsup.

curried eggplant

1 small eggplant, about 4 ounces
Oil for frying
6 to 7 tablespoons fine yellow
    cornmeal or flour
½ teaspoon salt
1 teaspoon crushed red-pepper flakes
    or ⅛ teaspoon chili powder
1 teaspoon curry powder
2 egg whites, beaten stiff

Cut eggplant into 1½-inch cubes.
Heat oil in medium saucepan to 375°F.
Mix cornmeal, salt, and spices.
Coat eggplant cubes with egg white; roll in cornmeal mixture. Fry eggplant until golden, about 1 minute. Drain on paper toweling. Sprinkle with salt. Serve immediately as a side dish.

indian okra

1 pound okra
4 tablespoons oil
2 teaspoons cumin
1 teaspoon salt
1 teaspoon turmeric
½ teaspoon cayenne
1 teaspoon ground coriander

Cut okra into thin slices.
Heat oil. Add cumin, salt, turmeric, and cayenne. Add okra; stir quickly until covered with oil. Cover; cook over low heat 5 minutes. Stir again; cook 10 minutes. Add coriander.

green-pepper sauté

2 large green (or red) peppers, cut
    into chunks
Boiling water
Butter or oil
Pepper
Soy sauce

Cut peppers; cook in boiling water about 2 minutes. Drain; sauté in butter or oil until just beginning to turn brown. Sprinkle with pepper and soy sauce.

rutabaga strips

1½ cups ¼-inch strips rutabaga
1 tablespoon butter or margarine
½ cup water
1 chicken bouillon cube
1 tablespoon sugar

Combine all ingredients in saucepan. Cook, covered, until rutabaga is tender, about 15 minutes.

Note: Use ½ cup chicken broth instead of bouillon cube and water, if desired.

delicious spinach

1 pound fresh spinach, washed, cut
    into 2-inch pieces
2 tablespoons oil
Salt to taste
1 small can bamboo shoots
8 fresh mushrooms, sliced
¼ cup chicken broth

Wash spinach; cut into pieces.
Heat oil in wok or skillet. Add salt and spinach; stir-fry 2 minutes. Add bamboo shoots, mushrooms, and chicken broth; mix. Cover; simmer about 2 minutes or until heated through.

stuffed sweet potato

1 good-sized sweet potato
3 tablespoons canned meat
1 small onion, finely chopped
1 tablespoon butter
1 tomato
1 sprig parsley

Cut sweet potato in half; scoop out center.
Mix canned meat, sautéed onion, and butter. Stuff sweet-potato shell with mixture. Garnish with tomato and parsley.

curried green tomatoes

2 tablespoons minced onions
2 tablespoons butter
1 teaspoon curry powder
Green tomatoes, sliced or chopped
Salt and pepper

Fry onion in butter until yellow. Add curry powder and tomatoes; cook slowly until well heated. Season with salt and pepper.

zucchini omelet

zucchini omelet

An Italian variation of the omelet. Excellent to serve as a light supper accompanied by a salad and hot garlic bread.

½ cup thinly sliced zucchini
2 slices onion
2 tablespoons butter
3 eggs
3 tablespoons water
¼ teaspoon basil or thyme
½ teaspoon salt
1/8 teaspoon freshly ground pepper
2 tablespoon diced fresh tomato
1 tablespoon grated Parmesan or
       Romato cheese

Sauté zucchini and onion in 1 tablespoon butter in small skillet until tender.

Combine eggs, water, basil, salt, and pepper in bowl; beat just until egg yolks and whites are blended.

Melt remaining butter in omelet pan. Add zucchini mixture to egg mixture; pour into hot omelet pan. Working with side of fork, lightly pull thickened edge away from side of pan, allowing soft parts to flow underneath. Cook until bottom is set but top is still moist. Loosen edges one last time. Sprinkle tomato and cheese over omelet; broil 6 inches from source of heat until cheese melts and top is lightly browned.

stuffed zucchini

2 zucchini, approximately 8 inches
   long
¼ pound lean ground beef
1 tablespoon dry bread crumbs
1 teaspoon catsup
½ teaspoon Worcestershire sauce
1 tablespoon instant minced onion

1 tablespoon chopped parsley
1 teaspoon celery salt
1 teaspoon oregano
Dash of garlic powder
Dash of pepper
1 egg, beaten
4 tablespoons Parmesan cheese

Wash zucchini. Cut off ends; halve lengthwise. Drop into pot of boiling water; cook until slightly tender. Plunge zucchini into cold water. Allow to cool; drain. Scoop out pulp with spoon, leaving shell about ¼ inch thick. Drain shells on paper towels. Chop zucchini pulp. Add all remaining ingredients except cheese; mix. Heap mixture into zucchini shells; sprinkle with cheese. Arrange in baking dish containing ½ cup water. Bake, uncovered, in 350°F oven 30 minutes.

stuffed zucchini

zucchini and tomato kabobs

2 medium-size zucchini
Cherry tomatoes
Melted butter
2 tablespoons grated Parmesan
    cheese
½ teaspoon oregano
Salt and pepper

Parboil zucchini 5 minutes in 2 cups salted water. Remove; cut each into 4 chunks. Thread alternately with cherry tomatoes on small skewer. Baste with hot butter. Cook 8 inches above hot coals about 10 minutes. Turn; baste frequently. Sprinkle with cheese, salt, and pepper.

tomato scramble

4 tomatoes, sliced
3 tablespoons oil
2 onions, sliced

3 eggs
1 tablespoon milk
Salt and pepper

Fry tomatoes in oil; set aside.
Add onions to same pan; cook until lightly browned. Remove from pan.
Beat eggs thoroughly with milk and seasonings. Pour into pan with oil; lower heat. Top with tomatoes and onions. Cook until eggs are set, stirring mixture gently.

fruit and vegetable casserole

2 eggs, separated
½ cup milk
½ teaspoon coarse salt
2 teaspoons sugar
¼ teaspoon nutmeg
¼ teaspoon cinnamon
1 cup cottage cheese
2 slices whole-wheat bread, diced
1 apple, peeled, diced
1 peach, peeled, diced
1 zucchini, unpeeled, coarsely grated
1 carrot, peeled, coarsely grated

In medium bowl beat yolks thick. Add milk, salt, sugar, nutmeg, cinnamon, cottage cheese, and bread; mix well. Fold in fruits and vegetables.
Beat egg whites stiff but not dry. Fold in fruit and vegetable mixture. Pour into well-greased 1½-quart baking idsh. Bake in 350°F oven about 45 minutes.
Serve casserole hot, with topping of yogurt or sour cream if desired.

mixed chinese vegetables

mixed chinese vegetables

5 large dried Chinese mushrooms
1 cup lukewarm water
5 ounces green cabbage
4 ounces carrots
4 ounces cucumber
5 ounces canned bamboo shoots
4 tablespoons sesame-seed oil

2 ounces frozen peas
½ cup hot chicken broth
2 tablespoons soy sauce
Salt
Pinch of sugar
Pinch of monosodium glutamate
    (MSG)

Soak mushrooms in water 30 minutes.
Shred cabbage.
Cut carrots, cucumber, and bamboo shoots into julienne strips.
Cube mushrooms.
Heat oil in skillet. Add cabbage; cook 2 minutes. Add mushrooms, cucumber,
carrots, bamboo shoots, and peas. Pour in chicken broth. Season with soy sauce,
salt, sugar, and MSG. Simmer over low heat 15 minutes. Serve immediately.

63

chinese fried vegetables

Oil for cooking
½ cup diagonally sliced celery
4 ounces bamboo shoots
4 ounces water chestnuts, sliced
3 scallions, sliced into 1-inch pieces
½ cup fresh mushrooms
1 cup bean sprouts, fresh or canned
Soy sauce to taste

Heat oil in skillet or wok. Add celery, bamboo shoots, and water chestnuts; stir-fry 2 minutes. Add scallions, mushrooms, and bean sprouts; stir-fry 1 minute or until heated through. Sprinkle with soy sauce to taste. Serve immediately.

marinated vegetables

¼ cup lemon juice
¼ cup salad oil
1 envelope French salad-dressing mix
½ cup water
1 cup raw carrot sticks
1 cup raw zucchini sticks
1 cup cauliflower florets
Lettuce leaves
Cottage cheese

Combine lemon juice, oil, and salad-dressing mix in cruet or jar with tight-fitting lid. Cover; shake well. Add water; shake again.

Combine prepared dressing and vegetables in saucepan. Bring to boil. Reduce heat; simmer 4 minutes. Cool slightly. Cover; chill about 3 hours; drain.

Serve on lettuce leaves, with cottage cheese.

Variation: 1 cup raw turnip sticks can be substituted for the cauliflower florets.

skillet vegetable dinner

1 cup rice
1 teaspoon salt
4 tablespoons oil
3 cups soup stock (2 or 3 bouillon
    cubes)
3 green peppers, sliced
2 teaspoons butter
1 medium eggplant, diced
7 sprigs parsley, chopped
1 teaspoon basil
1 teaspoon oregano
½ teaspoon garlic powder
Pepper
Onion rings
Juice of 2 lemons
4 ounces grated Parmesan or other
    cheese

Brown rice with salt and oil in large skillet. Stir frequently; keep on low flame about 10 to 15 minutes.

Meanwhile make stock; bring to boil.

Sauté peppers about 5 minutes in frying pan with butter. When rice is browned, add stock; stir. Add eggplant, peppers, parsley, basil, oregano, garlic powder, and pepper. Arrange onion rings on top. Add lemon juice. Cover; cook over low heat about 15 minutes, until rice and eggplant are tender. Sprinkle grated cheese over onions. Cover until cheese melts, or grill until cheese bubbles.

vegetable tempura

vegetables

Use a variety of the following, or whatever is available:

Eggplant
Green pepper
String beans
Mushrooms
Onion
Potato

tempura batter

1 egg
½ cup ice water
1 cup sifted flour

Oil for deep-frying

Slice vegetables into thin strips, keeping them separate; set aside.

Mix batter. Beat egg; add cold water and sifted flour all at once. Blend thoroughly, but do not overmix.

Heat oil in deep pan (or wok) until drop of water dropped into oil sizzles. Dip vegetables, few at a time, in batter; fry until crisp, using tongs to turn them. Take out of pan or wok with slotted spoon. Drain on paper towels. Dip vegetables in soy sauce before enjoying.

poultry

Two can be tempted with everything from Rock Cornish Hens to Stuffed Chicken Legs. Poultry lends itself well to the table for two as it can be purchased in small quantities and then tastily prepared.

chicken kiev

4 chicken breasts, boned, skinned	1 teaspoon Worcestershire sauce
½ cup butter or margarine, melted	½ cup sour cream
2 scallions, diced	1 egg
2 tablespoons chopped parsley	½ cup flour
1 teaspoon salt	1 cup bread crumbs
Dash of pepper	Fat for deep-frying

Lightly salt chicken; pound until flat.

Mix butter, scallions, parsley, salt, pepper, and Worcestershire sauce. Put 1 tablespoon of mixture at one end of breasts. Tuck in ends; roll. Secure with twine or toothpicks. (Can freeze at this point, if desired.)

Blend sour cream with egg.

Coat rolls with flour. Dip into sour cream–egg mixture; roll in bread crumbs. Chill about 30 minutes.

Remove twine or picks. Fry in deep fat (350°F) about 5 minutes. To use as an hors d'oeuvre, halve breasts.

chicken kiev

broiled spring chicken

Deceptively easy to prepare.

2 small broilers
Salt and pepper to taste

½ cup melted butter
4 tablespoons lemon juice

Remove wing tips from broilers; split from necks through breasts, leaving backs together. Place on chopping board; flatten with rolling pin. Season with salt and pepper. Place skin-side-up on rack in broiler pan.

Combine butter and lemon juice; brush broilers with mixture.

Place broiler pan 3 or 4 inches from source of heat; broil 2 minutes. Lower pan to about 10 inches from source of heat; broil about 40 minutes or until broilers are tender, turning frequently and basting with butter mixture each time.

Place chicken on platter; garnish with endive.

broiled spring chicken

chicken and ham in mushroom sauce

2 whole chicken breasts, skinned,
   boned
Salt and pepper
2 slices boiled ham
2 slices Swiss cheese
¼ cup whole-berry cranberry sauce
1 egg, well beaten
Flour
2 tablespoons butter or margarine
1 small onion, minced
1 can (2½ ounces) sliced mushrooms,
   drained
½ cup condensed cream of chicken
   soup, undiluted
1 tablespoon dry white wine
   (optional)

Pound whole chicken breasts between 2 sheets of waxed paper. Sprinkle with salt and pepper. Place 1 ham and 1 cheese slice on each chicken breast. Spoon 2 tablespoons cranberry sauce on each cheese slice. Fold in sides of chicken breast; roll up. Dip rolls in egg, then in flour.

Heat butter in skillet. Brown chicken rolls seam-side-down first, then on all sides. Add onion, mushrooms, soup, and wine. Stir to blend; cover. Simmer over low heat 20 to 25 minutes, stirring occasionally.

chicken with rice

This is a quick, tasty dish—excellent for using up leftover chicken.

2 tablespoons oil
2 medium onions, diced
1 green pepper, diced
2 cups cooked rice
2 cups diced cooked chicken breast
Soy sauce to taste
Dash of ginger

Heat oil in large skillet; brown onion. Add remaining ingredients; stir frequently while cooking over moderate heat 20 minutes.

crumb-topped chicken

1⅔ cups chopped cooked chicken
¾ cup chopped cooked ham
1¼ cups white sauce
Salt and pepper
Nutmeg
2 tablespoons butter
3 tablespoons fine bread crumbs

Remove skin and bone from chicken; chop meat. Add ham to chicken. Moisten mixture well with sauce. Season well; add little nutmeg.

Butter 6 deep scallop shells or an entree dish. Fill with mixture. Sprinkle evenly with bread crumbs; place butter shavings on top. Bake in fairly hot (375–400°F) oven until golden brown. Serve hot.

moo goo gai pan (chicken with pea pods)

1 pound boned chicken, cut into
     strips
3 tablespoons soy sauce
2 onions, sliced
4 stalks celery, cut into 1-inch strips
1 can Chinese vegetables
1 can mushrooms, drained (reserve
     liquid)
1 tablespoon monosodium glutamate
     (MSG)
½ cup water
2 chicken bouillon cubes
2 tablespoons cornstarch
1 tablespoon water
1 box frozen pea pods

Sauté chicken in 2 tablespoons soy sauce 5 minutes. Remove to dish.

Add onions, celery, Chinese vegetables, mushrooms, and MSG to pan.

Combine liquid from mushrooms with ½ cup water, remaining soy sauce, and bouillon cubes. Add to pan; cook 15 minutes. Add chicken; cook 5 minutes. (If thick sauce is desired, mix cornstarch with 1 tablespoon water. Add to pot; stir.) Add pea pods; cook 3 to 4 minutes.

Very good served with rice.

skewered chicken pieces

marinade

1 cup soy sauce
1 cup sake (rice wine) or sherry

3 tablespoons sugar, or little less
2 teaspoons freshly ground pepper

1½ to 2 pounds chicken meat, cut
into cubes

Mix together soy sauce, sake, sugar, and pepper; bring to boil.
Marinate chicken in marinade 30 minutes. Put chicken pieces on skewer and broil; or, put on grill or hibachi. Brush with extra marinade during cooking, turning to brown well on all sides.

chicken and vegetable balls

12 ounces leftover cooked chicken,
chopped
2 bamboo shoots, cut into very thin
strips
4 mushrooms, chopped
2 small carrots, finely chopped
1 egg, beaten

1 teaspoon soy sauce
1 teaspoon sugar
3 cups chicken stock
4 tablespoons soy sauce
1 tablespoon sugar

Combine chicken, bamboo shoots, mushrooms, carrots, egg, 1 teaspoon soy sauce, and 1 teaspoon sugar. Mix very well. Form into balls. Drop meatballs into boiling chicken stock to which 4 tablespoons soy sauce and 1 tablespoon sugar have been added. Simmer about 8 minutes.
Serve meatballs hot or cold. The chicken-stock mixture is also served hot poured into individual bowls.

chicken sukiyaki

2 cups chicken stock
1 cup sugar
1 cup soy sauce
1 pound chicken meat, cut into
bite-size pieces

8 large mushrooms, sliced
3 carrots, sliced diagonally,
parboiled
6 scallions, cut into 2-inch lengths

Mix chicken stock with sugar and soy sauce. Bring to boil. Add half of chicken; simmer about 12 minutes. Add half of remaining ingredients; simmer 3 minutes. Serve this with rice; repeat the process.

stuffed chicken legs

2 cold cooked chicken legs
1 tablespoon oil
2 tablespoons bread crumbs
½ teaspoon mixed herbs
1 teaspoon chopped parsley
2 slices blanched onion
½ teaspoon grated lemon rind
Cayenne pepper
Salt
1 egg
4 slices bacon
2 slices buttered toast
Parsley sprigs

Cut each leg in two at joint. Moisten with oil.

Mix bread crumbs, finely chopped herbs, chopped parsley, and onion in bowl. Add lemon rind, cayenne pepper, and salt; moisten with egg.

Drain chicken legs; cover each with stuffing. Wrap in slices of bacon; tie or skewer securely. Place on greased baking tray; cook in moderate (350°F) oven 20 minutes.

Dish chicken on trimmed slices of toast; garnish with parsley. Serve hot.

chicken livers

This recipe can be prepared ahead and put in refrigerator. Fry when needed.

½ pound chicken livers
6 strips bacon, cut in half
12 slices onion
12 mushroom caps
2 eggs
2 tablespoons cognac or brandy
Salt and pepper
Bread crumbs
Butter or margarine for frying

Alternately put on skewer piece of liver wrapped in bacon, slice of onion, and mushroom cap, until skewer is full. (A 6-inch skewer will do.) Brush with egg beaten with cognac, salt, and pepper. Roll in bread crumbs. Cook in frying pan with butter until golden brown on all sides.

simmered chicken livers

1 pound chicken livers
1 cup soy sauce
3 tablespoons white wine
1½ cups water
3 tablespoons sugar
1 tablespoon freshly grated ginger or
    ½ tablespoon ground ginger
8 scallions, cut into 1-inch pieces

Cut livers in half.

Mix together soy sauce, wine, water, sugar, and ginger; bring to boil. Add livers; boil slowly until most liquid is absorbed. Add scallions; cook 2 minutes.

pineapple duck

1 duck, about 4 pounds
4 slices canned pineapple
1 large green pepper, cut into 1-inch
    squares
2 tablespoons oil
1 teaspoon salt
¼ teaspoon pepper
½ teaspoon monosodium glutamate
    (MSG)
1 tablespoon soy sauce
1 tablespoon cornstarch mixed with 2
    tablespoons cold water

Clean and quarter duck. Cover with boiling water; simmer gently until tender. Remove from broth; let duck drain. Reserve broth.

Cut each pineapple slice into 8 pieces.

Cut pepper into squares.

Preheat skillet; add oil. Place pieces of duck in skillet, along with salt and pepper. Brown gently, turning frequently. When browned, add pineapple and green pepper; stir-fry few seconds. Add broth, MSG, and soy sauce. Cover; simmer about 10 minutes. Thicken slightly with cornstarch mixture.

Serve duck with rice.

skillet game hen

1 fresh Cornish hen (about 1¼
    pounds)
¼ cup butter
Salt and pepper
⅓ cup clear fat-free chicken broth

Split hen in half. Cut off narrow central spinal bone; discard. With cleaver, flatten each half on both sides. Cut joint (but not all the way through) between wing and breast so wing will lie flat.

Melt butter in heavy medium-size skillet over medium heat. Add hen halves; brown thoroughly on both sides, about 10 minutes. Cover tightly; cook over moderate heat, turning as necessary, until tender, 20 to 25 minutes. Remove hen. Sprinkle with salt and pepper; keep hot.

Add chicken broth to butter and drippings in skillet; stirring constantly, boil just until reduced and slightly thickened. Pour over hen.

seafood

Fish and seafood of all kinds assume large places on many menus today since they are included in diet lists from low calorie to low-cholesterol diets. Enhance the bounty of the sea with the new and delicious recipes included here.

maryland crab cakes

1-pound can crab meat
2 eggs
2 tablespoons horseradish mustard
¼ teaspoon salt
⅛ teaspoon pepper
5 drops Tabasco
1 onion, minced
1 tablespoon chopped parsley
Cracker crumbs
Fat for frying

Combine all ingredients except crumbs and fat; mix together lightly. Form into desired-size cakes. Do not pack firmly. Pat cakes into crumbs.

Heat 1½ inches fat in heavy skillet. Brown cakes on both sides until golden. Serve immediately.

seafood and onions in miso sauce

1 pound small onions
1 cup small clams or scallops
Vinegar for soaking clams

miso sauce

2 tablespoons sugar
2 tablespoons dashi
4 tablespoons miso
2 tablespoons vinegar

Slice onions; boil until just tender.

Soak clams in small amount of vinegar while onions are boiling. If using scallops, salt lightly before soaking in vinegar.

Make Miso Sauce. Add sugar and dashi to miso; blend very well. Stir in vinegar.

Drain clams; add, with onions, to sauce. Serve immediately.

buttered crab

2 anchovy fillets
½ pint white wine
Pinch of grated nutmeg
1 cup white bread crumbs
Salt and pepper
2 good-size crabs, cooked, flaked
3 tablespoons butter
Slices of buttered toast

Mash anchovies in wine. Add nutmeg and bread crumbs; season to taste. Bring gently to boil; simmer 5 minutes.

Mix the crab meat with butter. Add to hot wine mixture; cook 4 minutes.

Serve crab with toast.

crab dumplings

12 ounces fresh crab meat, or frozen
    if fresh is unavailable
3 tablespoons bread or cracker
    crumbs
1 egg, beaten
Flour for hands

batter

1 cup flour
1 egg
1 cup water

Oil for frying

Thoroughly mix crab meat, crumbs, and egg. Make small balls with floured hands; refrigerate about 30 minutes.

Meanwhile make batter of flour, egg, and water; blend until well-mixed. It may remain lumpy.

Heat oil. Dip balls into batter; fry in hot oil. Drain on paper toweling.

Serve dumplings with soy sauce if desired.

fish in coconut sauce

1¼ cups coconut cream	1 small onion
1 medium fish or 1 can mackerel	1 teaspoon salt

Pour little coconut cream into pot.

Cut cleaned, filleted fish into 2 or 3 pieces. Add remaining coconut cream. If canned fish is used, drain off oil. Add onion and salt; slowly bring to boil. Cook slowly until fish is done, 15 to 20 minutes.

Serve fish hot with lemon juice.

eel kabobs

2 eels, about 1 pound each

marinade

¾ cup rice wine or sherry
3 teaspoons honey
5 tablespoons soy sauce

Skin eels; cut off heads. With very sharp knife remove eel fillets from bone; cut into 1½-inch pieces. Place in deep bowl.

Combine rice wine, honey, and soy sauce; heat. Pour marinade over eel pieces; let marinate 30 minutes.

Light coals in barbecue grill; wait until white-hot. Thread eel pieces on metal skewers; place on grill. Turn skewers occasionally; baste with marinade. Grill 15 minutes. (This can also be done under oven broiler or on hibachi.)

eel kabobs

baked fish

1 pound fish fillets (sole, flounder,
    or red snapper)
1 tablespoon chopped parsley
1 tablespoon lemon juice
½ teaspoon seasoned salt
2 tablespoons olive oil
1 medium onion, thinly sliced
1 clove garlic, minced
1 large tomato, chopped
3 slices lemon
2 tablespoons white wine

Arrange fish in 9-inch-square baking dish. Sprinkle with parsley, lemon juice, and salt.

Heat oil in small frypan. Fry onion and garlic until limp. Cover fish with onion mixture, including oil from pan. Top onion mixture with chopped tomato. Place lemon slices around tomato. Pour wine over. Bake at 350°F 30 to 35 minutes or until fish flakes.

baked fish

pineapple fish

1- to 1½-pound fish fillet
1 teaspoon salt
Pepper to taste
1 egg
1 cup cornstarch
Oil for deep frying
Sweet-and-Sour Sauce

Cut fish into 1 × 2-inch pieces.

Combine salt, pepper, and egg in mixing bowl; mix well. Add fish; toss to coat. Marinate 10 minutes. Coat fish heavily with cornstarch.

Heat oil in a 10- or 12-inch skillet, to a depth of 1 inch, over high heat. Fry fish on both sides until light brown. Arrange fish on platter. Keep in warm (about 200°F) oven while preparing sauce.

To prepare ahead: Follow recipe for frying fish, but remove from skillet when very light brown. Reheat fish in 400°F oven 5 to 9 minutes.

sweet-and-sour sauce

1 tablespoon vegetable oil
2 whole cloves garlic
1 teaspoon shredded fresh gingerroot
     or ¼ teaspoon ground ginger
½ cup brown sugar
½ cup cider vinegar
2 tablespoons soy sauce
1 cup syrup from canned pineapple
½ cup water
2 tablespoons cornstarch dissolved
     in 4 tablespoons water
1 20-ounce can pineapple
     chunks, drained
1 green pepper, thinly sliced

Heat oil in saucepan over medium heat. Brown garlic and ginger; blend in brown sugar, vinegar, soy sauce, pineapple syrup, and water. Remove garlic. Bring to boil. Stir in dissolved cornstarch; cook, stirring constantly, until sauce is thickened. Mix in pineapple and pepper. Pour sauce over fish. Serve immediately.

steamed whole fish

1 pound whole fish (flounder, pike, trout, or sea bass)
1 teaspoon salt
½ teaspoon freshly ground pepper
¼ teaspoon powdered ginger
3 cups water
2 teaspoons mixed pickling spices (more, if you like it spicier)

2 bay leaves
2 cloves garlic, halved
2 tablespoons chopped scallion
Lemon slices
Tomato
Parsley

Have fish scaled, cleaned, and head removed if you prefer. Lightly score skin so seasonings will flavor fish.

Combine salt, pepper, and ginger; rub on fish thoroughly.

Pour water into large frypan or wok; add pickling spices, bay leaves, garlic, and scallion. Place rack in pan so fish will be above liquid, to allow steam to circulate. Place fish on rack. Cover; let simmer approximately 30 minutes or until fish is tender.

Garnish fish with lemon slices, tomato, and parsley.

steamed whole fish

82

halibut cantonese

1½ pounds halibut, cut into small chunks
1 tablespoon oil
1 medium onion, chopped

sauce

1½ cups water
1 tablespoon oil
Pinch of salt
3 teaspoons soy sauce
1 teaspoon monosodium glutamate
    (MSG)
Pinch of freshly ground pepper
2 tablespoons cornstarch dissolved
    in 3 tablespoons water

2 cloves garlic, minced
1 scallion, sliced
1 tablespoon chopped celery
1 egg, beaten

Boil halibut in pot of water 2 minutes.
Heat oil in skillet; brown onion. Transfer fish to skillet.
Mix together sauce ingredients, except cornstarch and water. Pour sauce on fish. Add garlic, scallion, and celery. Cover skillet; simmer 2 minutes. Pour egg slowly into sauce, mixing constantly. Stir cornstarch into sauce. Cook until thickened.

mahi mahi

¼ pound butter
1½ pounds mahi-mahi steaks
    (halibut or sole)
1 teaspoon salad oil
¼ teaspoon garlic salt
1 teaspoon soy sauce
½ teaspoon lemon juice

Melt butter; pour over fish along with other ingredients. Marinate 30 minutes. Grill over charcoal until fish is "flake"-done. Fish could be broiled if you prefer.
Serve fish with lemon slices and parsley sprigs.

broiled lobsters

Use a really sharp knife to split the lobsters.

2 live lobsters, 1 pound each
1 tablespoon butter, melted
¼ teaspoon salt
Dash of white pepper
Dash of paprika
¼ cup butter, melted
1 tablespoon lemon juice

Place lobster on its back. Insert sharp knife between body shell and tail segment, cutting down to sever spinal cord. Cut in half lengthwise. Remove stomach, which is just back of head, and intestinal vein, which runs from stomach to tip of tail. Do not discard green liver and coral roe. Crack claws. Lay lobsters open as flat as possible on broiler pan. Brush with 1 tablespoon butter. Sprinkle with salt, pepper, and paprika. Broil about 4 inches from source of heat 12 to 15 minutes or until lightly browned.

Combine ¼ cup butter and lemon juice. Serve with lobsters.

deviled lobster

1 boiled lobster
Butter
3 tablespoons white bread crumbs
2 tablespoons white sauce or cream
Cayenne pepper
Few browned bread crumbs

Cut lobster in two lengthwise; remove meat carefully (half shell must be kept whole). Chop meat finely.

Melt 3 tablespoons butter; pour on lobster. Add white bread crumbs and sauce. Season rather highly with cayenne; mix well. Press mixture lightly into shells. Cover with browned bread crumbs; put 3 or 4 pieces butter on top. Bake about 20 minutes in moderate (350°F) oven. Serve hot or cold.

hong kong lobster

2 large lobster tails
2 tablespoons oil
½ teaspoon salt
1 small can button mushrooms,
    drained
½ cup thinly sliced bamboo shoots
½ cup thinly sliced celery
⅓ teaspoon sugar
1 teaspoon soy sauce
½ teaspoon monosodium
    glutamate (MSG)
1 cup chicken stock
1 tablespoon cornstarch
1 tablespoon water

Remove lobster meat from shells; slice into ½-inch pieces.

Place oil and salt in preheated skillet. Turn heat high. Bring oil to sizzling point. Add lobster; toss rapidly 2 minutes. Add remaining ingredients except cornstarch and water. Turn lightly until thoroughly mixed. Cover; cook at high heat 7 minutes; uncover. Gradually add cornstarch that has been smoothed into paste with water. Toss and cook over high heat until sauce is thickened.

maine boiled lobster

2 live lobsters, 1 pound each
3 quarts boiling water
3 tablespoons salt
Melted butter

Plunge lobsters headfirst into boiling salted water. Cover; return to boiling point. Simmer 20 minutes; drain. Place lobster on its back. With sharp knife cut in half lengthwise. Remove stomach, which is just back of head, and intestinal vein, which runs from stomach to top of tail. Do not discard green liver and coral roe— they are delicious. Crack claws.

Serve lobster with melted butter.

lobster newburg

½ stick butter
1½ heaping tablespoons flour
1 can evaporated milk
½ cup cream
Juice of ½ lemon
1 egg, lightly beaten
1 pound lobster, cut into lumps
1 wine-glass sherry

Place butter in top of double boiler over low fire. Add flour; stir well.
Add milk, cream, and lemon juice to egg. Add to flour and butter mixture. Place over low heat; stir constantly. When well blended, add lobster. Add sherry just before serving.

landlubber's spiced lobsters

Although an "old salt" might disdain "fancying up" his lobsters this way, you'll find this recipe a favorite with many.

1 cup vinegar
2 carrots, sliced
2 stalks celery, sliced
1 onion, sliced
1 lemon, sliced
3 tablespoons salt
½ cup mixed pickling spice
3 quarts boiling water
2 live 1-pound lobsters

Add vinegar, vegetables, lemon, and seasonings to boiling water. Cover; simmer 30 minutes. Plunge lobsters headfirst into water. Cover; return to boiling point. Simmer 15 minutes. Remove from heat; cool in liquid. Drain, split, and clean.

mussels florentine

12 ounces spinach
12 fresh or canned mussels
3 tablespoons butter
4 tablespoons flour

¼ cups milk
Seasoning
A little grated cheese

Cook spinach.

Put shellfish in small saucepan; add their liquor, previously strained through muslin. Poach 2 to 3 minutes, until edges just begin to ruffle slightly; remove from heat.

Melt butter in saucepan. Stir in flour; cook 2 minutes. Add milk; stir until boiling. Boil 3 minutes. Cool slightly. Add shellfish and their liquor.

Drain spinach; spread over bottom of casserole dish. Pour sauce on top; sprinkle with finely grated cheese. Brown lightly under broiler. Serve immediately.

shad and roe veronique

1 shad fillet
½ pair shad roe (use larger portion)
Salt and freshly ground
       pepper to taste
2 tablespoons butter
1 tablespoon finely chopped shallots
½ cup fresh or canned white seedless
       grapes, preferably fresh
1 cup heavy cream
Juice of ½ lemon

Preheat oven to 400°F.

Sprinkle shad fillet and roe with salt and pepper.

Rub bottom of baking dish with butter. Sprinkle with shallots. Arrange shad fillet skin-side-down on baking dish. Do not open up flaps of fillet where bones were removed. Arrange roe half next to fillet.

If fresh seedless grapes are available, remove from stems; rinse and drain well. Scatter them around fish and roe. Cover with buttered waxed paper; cook on top of stove until it sizzles. Place dish in oven; bake 15 minutes. Remove from oven.

Pour liquid from fish into small skillet. Do not add grapes. Cook liquid until almost evaporated. Add cream; cook down over high heat. Pour any additional liquid that accumulates around fish and roe into cream sauce. Cook cream mixture over high heat until syrupy and saucelike, about 5 minutes. Put sauce through sieve, preferably the sort known in French kitchens as a chinoise. Press sauce through with back of a spoon.

If canned grapes are used, drain them; add them or cooked fresh grapes to sauce. Reheat sauce; add lemon juice.

salmon molds

7¾-ounce can red salmon
2 tablespoons sour cream
Minced onion to taste
Paprika

Open can of salmon; leave the bones — they are edible and nutritious. Mash fine; mix in sour cream and onion. Turn into 2 buttered 6-ounce custard cups; sprinkle with paprika. Bake in a preheated 350°F oven until set, about 20 minutes. Loosen edges; unmold. Turn right-side-up if you like.

broiled scallops

Good served with rice.

1 pound fresh scallops
Melted butter
Lemon juice
Freshly ground pepper (optional)
Soy sauce

Place scallops on broiler; brush with melted butter mixed with lemon juice. Sprinkle with pepper; broil just until done. Sprinkle with soy sauce.

boiled shrimp

2 ounces cabbage, thinly sliced
8 ounces cucumbers, peeled, cut into ¼-inch cubes
8 ounces shrimp

sauce

2 teaspoons horseradish
¼ cup soy sauce

Dip cabbage quickly into boiling water; let dry.
Peel and slice cucumbers.
Boil shrimp in salted water about 5 minutes.
Combine horseradish and soy sauce.
Serve cabbage, cucumbers, and shrimp in small bowls. Dip shrimp into sauce.

shrimp-in-the-shell

Messy, but such good eating!

1 pound shrimp
¼ cup butter
2 cloves garlic
½ teaspoon salt

Wash shrimp in cold water. Drain; do not shell.
Melt butter in small saucepan over low heat.
Peel and crush garlic; add to butter.
Arrange unshelled shrimp in one layer in shallow pan. Pour butter–garlic mixture over shrimp. Sprinkle with salt. Broil about 4 inches from high heat 10 minutes. Shells will be pink and shrimp cooked through when done.
Serve drained shrimp in shells with plenty of paper napkins. Eaters remove shells. Serve remaining juices as sauce for dunking shrimp.

butterfly shrimp cantonese

1 pound shrimp
½ pound sliced bacon

sauce

1 large can tomato sauce
Juice of ½ lemon
⅓ cup brown sugar
⅓ cup vinegar
1 tablespoon Worcestershire sauce
3 pieces sour salt

Shredded lettuce
Chopped green onions

Split shrimp. Remove shell; devein. Open butterfly-style; flatten.
Cut bacon strips in half. Fry on low until golden to light brown, not crisp; drain. Wrap each shrimp in bacon; roll. Secure with toothpicks. Bake in 350°F oven 10 to 15 minutes.
Combine all sauce ingredients; cook 10 minutes.
Add baked shrimp to sauce; cook 5 minutes.
Put lettuce in bottom of serving bowl. Pour shrimp and sauce over lettuce. Top with green onions.
Serve shrimp with cooked rice. Can also be used as an hors d'oeuvre.

shrimp with marinara sauce

1 pound shrimp
1 quart water
Salt to taste
1 bay leaf
1 slice lemon

marinara sauce

2 tablespoons olive oil
½ cup chopped onion
1 clove garlic, minced
1½ cups Italian-style peeled
    plum tomatoes
¼ cup tomato puree
½ teaspoon sugar
½ teaspoon crumbled dried
    sweet basil
Salt and pepper

garnish

2 tablespoons dry bread crumbs
2 tablespoons grated Parmesan
    cheese
1 tablespoon finely chopped parsley

Peel and devein shrimp.

Combine water, salt, bay leaf, and lemon in large saucepan; bring to boil. Add shrimp; bring water rapidly to boil. Cook 5 minutes; drain.

Prepare sauce. Heat oil in heavy skillet. Add onion and garlic; sauté until tender. Break up tomatoes; add tomatoes, tomato puree, and seasonings to onion and garlic. Reduce heat to low; cook, uncovered, 20 minutes.

Place shrimp in lightly greased au gratin dish. Top with sauce.

Combine bread crumbs, cheese, and parsley; sprinkle over shrimp and sauce.

Preheat oven to 450°F; bake 10 minutes.

shrimp with marinara sauce

sesame shrimp

½ cup sesame seeds, toasted
1 pound shrimp, cleaned
Salt
Freshly ground black pepper
6 tablespoons melted butter

Place sesame seeds in ungreased skillet over low heat; stir until browned. Set aside.

Sprinkle shrimp lightly with salt and pepper. Dip in melted butter; roll in toasted sesame seeds. Skewer shrimp; grill approximately 8 minutes over grill or hibachi, turning frequently to brown evenly.

golden shrimp

12 large fresh shrimp

marinade

3 tablespoons soy sauce
1 tablespoon rice wine or sherry
Ginger to taste, either ground or grated gingerroot

Cornstarch
Oil for frying

Rinse shrimp.

Mix together soy sauce, rice wine, and ginger. Add shrimp; marinate 30 minutes. Drain well. Sprinkle shrimp with cornstarch; set aside 3 minutes.

Heat oil in deep fryer or frying pan; fry shrimp.

Shrimp can be left whole for a main course or cut into approximately 3 pieces each for an appetizer.

shrimp and bean sprouts

1 cup diagonally sliced celery
1 cup sliced fresh mushrooms
½ cup sliced scallions
Oil for cooking

½ pound fresh bean sprouts
½ pound cooked shrimp
Soy sauce to taste

Prepare celery, mushrooms, and scallions.

Heat oil in skillet or wok; stir-fry celery until it turns bright green. Add mushrooms and scallions; stir-fry 1 minute. Add bean sprouts and shrimp; toss lightly until heated through, approximately 2 minutes. Sprinkle with soy sauce.

shrimp with mandarin oranges

2 teaspoons sherry
1 teaspoon cornstarch
½ pound shrimp, cleaned
Oil for cooking

½ cup drained canned mandarin-
orange segments
¼ teaspoon sugar
¼ teaspoon salt

Mix together sherry and cornstarch; marinate shrimp in mixture 5 minutes.

Heat oil in skillet or wok, enough to cover bottom of pan; stir-fry shrimp just until color changes. Add orange segments, sugar, and salt; stir-fry just until heated through, no more than 1 minute.

hot-mustard shrimp

3 tablespoons powdered mustard
¼ teaspoon salt
1 teaspoon sugar
1 teaspoon horseradish

¾ cup flat beer
1 pound shrimp, cleaned
4 tablespoons melted butter
Duck sauce (or plum sauce)

Mix mustard, salt, sugar, and horseradish together. Add enough beer to make smooth paste. Gradually add rest of beer to make it thin; let stand 1 hour. If it becomes too thick, add more beer or cold water.

Dip shrimp in mustard sauce. Skewer; brush with melted butter. Grill on hibachi or grill approximately 8 minutes. Turn frequently for even browning.

Serve shrimp with duck sauce.

shrimp provencal

8 ounces frozen or fresh shrimp
　(weight when peeled)
2 tablespoons butter
1 to 2 tablespoons olive oil
1 small onion, thinly sliced
½ clove garlic, crushed

2 tomatoes
2 to 3 large mushrooms
Seasoning
2 teaspoons chopped parsley
Lemon juice

Separate frozen shrimp.

Heat butter and oil together; fry onion and garlic.

Skin and slice tomatoes.

Slice mushrooms.

Add tomatoes, mushrooms, and shrimp to onion; fry together until just tender. Season well; add parsley and lemon juice. Serve at once.

For a more substantial dish serve on a bed of boiled rice.

scampi

20 shrimp, split or butterflied
½ stick butter or margarine
2 cloves garlic, crushed
1 teaspoon parsley flakes
2 teaspoons lemon juice

1 teaspoon salt
½ cup dry white wine
1 teaspoon prepared mustard
Lemon wedges

Place shrimp on broiler pan.

Combine remaining ingredients, except lemon wedges; brush over shrimp. Broil 5 minutes, 3 inches from heat.

Serve shrimp over rice, with lemon wedges. Pour remaining sauce over rice.

shewered shrimp

4 large shelled shrimp

sauce

1 tablespoon (or less) salt
4 tablespoons soy sauce
¾ tablespoon rice wine or
  sherry
¼ teaspoon freshly grated
  ginger
Asparagus tips

Cut shrimp into bite-size pieces.
Make sauce. Blend together salt, soy sauce, rice wine (sake), and ginger.
Dip shrimp into sauce; place on skewers.
Dip asparagus tips into sauce; place on skewers. Broil in oven, basting with sauce; or grill or use hibachi.

sole portuguese

1 medium-size sole
2 tablespoons butter
1 shallot, finely chopped
1 teaspoon finely chopped parsley
½ teaspoon anchovy extract
Salt and pepper
1 onion
2 or 3 tomatoes
2 teaspoons grated Parmesan cheese
2 teaspoons browned bread crumbs
Extra butter

Skin sole; make incision down center as for filleting. Raise flesh from bone on each side as far as possible.

Mix butter, shallot, parsley, and anchovy extract together well; stuff mixture inside sole. Place fish in buttered casserole; season. Arrange slices of onion and tomato alternately, overlapping each other, on top of fish; if less onion is preferred, surround each slice of tomato with single onion ring.

Mix together cheese and bread crumbs; sprinkle over fish. Place small pieces of butter on top; cover with lid. Bake about 20 minutes in moderate (350°F) oven.

Fillets of sole can be laid on a bed of stuffing and cooked the same way. Omit onion and tomato rings if desired.

sole fillet with shrimp sauce

½ pound fillet of sole or other
    mild-flavored fish
1 tablespoon lemon juice

shrimp sauce

½ of 10½-ounce can shrimp soup
1 tablespoon butter or margarine
¼ teaspoon cornstarch
1 teaspoon milk

Chopped parsley

Place fillets in frypan with lemon juice; cover. Cook over low heat 15 minutes.
Slowly heat soup and butter in heavy saucepan, stirring frequently.
Mix cornstarch with milk; stir into soup. Cook until thickened, about 5 minutes.
To serve, pour Shrimp Sauce over fish; garnish with chopped parsley.

trout in foil

10-ounce package frozen boned
    rainbow trout (2 whole), thawed
Salt and pepper to taste
2 tablespoons butter, cut small
4 small or 2 large scallions,
    thinly sliced
1 green pepper, thinly sliced

Dry trout with paper towels; place each in center of sheet of foil large enough to make well-sealed package. Sprinkle insides of each fish with salt and pepper; stuff with butter, scallions, and green pepper. (It doesn't matter if some of vegetable is not enclosed.) Bring 2 long ends of foil up over trout so they meet; make drugstore fold; fold over ends several times. Place on small cookie sheet or in shallow pan. Bake in preheated 400°F oven 20 to 25 minutes.

cold trout treat

10-ounce package boned frozen rainbow trout (thawed)
¼ cup prepared dijon-style mustard
1½ teaspoons sugar
2 tablespoons olive oil
2 tablespoons white-wine vinegar
2 tablespoons (or more) minced fresh dill
Salad greens
Sliced tomatoes
Cucumbers

There will be 2 whole boned trout in package. Cut off heads, fins, and tails. Open each trout; cut in half lengthwise.

Pour 6 cups water into 12-inch skillet; bring to boil. Reduce heat to keep water at simmer. Add trout skin-side-down in single layer; water will cover them generously as they swell. Simmer, uncovered, until opaque through when tested with fork, 3 to 5 minutes. With slotted pancake turner, remove fillets; place them skin-side-up in single layer on kitchen tray to drain. Immediately skin fillets by inserting thin-bladed knife just under skin at wide end, then peeling off skin with your fingers; discard skin.

Whisk together mustard, sugar, oil, vinegar, and dill in small bowl.

Remove 2 fillets (they will be firm enough to pick up with your fingers) to serving platter. Spoon half the mustard sauce over them; it will run down. Top with remaining 2 fillets so each fish is assembled as if whole; spoon remaining sauce over top. Cover with plastic wrap; chill 12 to 24 hours to allow flavors to blend.

At serving time, garnish with salad greens, tomatoes, and cucumbers. Serve with French bread and sweet butter.

poached stuffed flounder

Celery (tops will do)
Onions
2 flounder fillets
1 cup moist bread crumbs
1 lemon
Salt and pepper

Start heating ½ inch water in large skillet.

Slice celery and onions to cover bottom. Lay 1 fillet skin-side-down on celery and onions. Spread crumbs thickly on fillet. Squeeze wedge of lemon over bread crumbs. Add salt and pepper. Lay second fillet skin-side-up on top. Cover or wrap skillet tightly with foil, poking hole for steam to escape. Cook slowly 15 to 20 minutes, until fish flakes easily.

Serve fish from skillet with spatula.

quick-and-easy creamed tuna

Delicious over baking powder biscuits, toast points, rice, noodles, or scones.

1 package cream of celery soup
    (can substitute cream of chicken
    or cream of mushroom soup)

2 cups water
1 6½-ounce can tuna, drained
3 tablespoons chopped onion

Heat dry soup with water.

Add tuna and onion; heat through, adding more water if mixture becomes too thick.

tuna gumbo

2 tablespoons sliced scallions
1 green pepper, diced
1 tablespoon butter or margarine
1 10½-ounce can condensed chicken gumbo soup
½ soup can tomato juice
½ soup can water
1 7-ounce can tuna packed in water, drained, flaked
Dash of pepper
Dash of thyme

Cook scallions and pepper in butter until tender. Stir in remaining ingredients. Heat; stir occasionally.

flounder stuffed with crab

1½- to 2-pound fresh flounder
Salt
½ pound backfin crab lumps
Lemon slices
Fresh parsley

Scrape white side and remove skin from dark side of flounder. Split down center all the way on dark side. Cut across top; turn flaps back. Sprinkle with salt; stuff with backfin crab lumps. Place on well-greased baking dish; bake in 350°F oven 20 minutes.

Garnish fish with lemon slices and fresh parsley to serve.

tuna cakes

tuna cakes

2 eggs
1 can (7 ounces) tuna, drained
1 small onion, finely chopped

4 slices bread, cubed (stale is fine)
Salt and pepper to taste

Beat eggs slightly in bowl. Add flaked tuna, onion, bread cubes, and seasonings; mix to moisten. Form into 4 to 6 patties; fry in skillet or on griddle until golden brown, turning once. Serve cakes with mayonnaise.

tuna casserole japanese

1 small can tuna
½ cup diced onion
½ cup diced celery
1 can bean sprouts, rinsed with cold
    water, drained

¼ cup diced green pepper
Soy sauce to taste

Drain tuna; mix with onion, celery, bean sprouts, pepper, and soy sauce. Place in casserole; bake at 350°F 30 minutes. Add additional soy sauce if needed.

fish timbales

1 pound halibut or salmon, flaked
2 eggs
½ pint cream
¼ pound chopped almonds
Salt
Pepper
Paprika
2 tablespoons butter, melted

Mix all ingredients together; put in buttered timbale or ring. Set in pan of hot water; bake 15 minutes.

Serve fish with cream sauce.

meats

You may expect to find recipes for beef, pork, veal and lamb here. But why not try tasty Beef Slices Peking or Steak Tartare. Your table for two will earn many compliments for the cook with these new and different recipes.

broiled filets mignons

broiled filets mignons

1¼-inch-thick filets mignons

Place filets on rack in broiling pan.

Set oven at broil; preheat several minutes. Place broiling pan in highest position in broiler; sear filets 2 to 3 minutes on each side. Lower pan to middle position; broil 2 minutes on each side for rare, 3 minutes and 30 seconds for medium, and 4 minutes for well done.

Serve filets on croutons or toast rounds, topped with flavored butter.

maitre d'hotel butter

½ cup softened butter
Strained juice of ½ lemon
Salt and pepper to season
1 heaping tablespoon chopped parsley leaves

Blend all ingredients in small mixing bowl. Shape mixture into round or square pat; refrigerate until ready to use. Cut into desired shapes.

101

steak japanese

2½ tablespoons soy sauce
2 filets mignons, about 12 ounces
    each
1 can bean sprouts, or 8 ounces fresh
3 tablespoons butter
2 tablespoons lemon juice
Sugar
Black pepper
4 ounces mandarin oranges (canned)
4 tablespoons oil

Sprinkle 2 tablespoons soy sauce over steaks. Rub in; let steaks marinate 1 hour.

Meanwhile drain canned bean sprouts; or, if using fresh, blanch, rinse with cold water, drain.

Heat 2 tablespoons butter in saucepan. Add bean sprouts; season with lemon juice, sugar, pepper, and remaining soy sauce. Simmer 5 minutes; keep warm.

Heat remaining butter in another small saucepan. Add drained oranges; heat through, about 2 minutes. Keep warm.

Heat oil in heavy skillet over high heat until light haze forms above it. Add steaks; quickly brown each side about ½ minute. Lower heat; cook steaks about 10 minutes on each side.

Arrange steaks on preheated platter. Garnish with bean sprouts and mandarin oranges. Serve immediately.

chinese pepper steak

Flank steak
2 tablespoons shortening
Salt and pepper
2 tablespoons diced onion
½ clove garlic, minced
2 green peppers, cut up

½ celery stalk, cut into chunks
½ cup beef bouillon
1 tablespoon cornstarch
2 tablespoons water
1 teaspoon soy sauce

Cut steak into slantwise 1/8-inch-thick slices. Brown in heavy skillet in shortening. Add salt and pepper, onion, garlic, green peppers, celery, and bouillon. Cover pan tightly; cook over moderate heat until meat and vegetables are tender but not limp, about 10 minutes.

Blend together cornstarch, water, and soy sauce. Add to meat; cook few more minutes, until juice thickens, stirring constantly.

Serve steak at once with hot rice.

beef slices peking

marinade

3 tablespoons soy sauce
1 tablespoon sherry

1 pound lean beef, sliced paper-thin	½ teaspoon powdered ginger
1 cup oil	2 tablespoons soy sauce
2 tablespoons flour	⅛ teaspoon ground anise
2 leeks, thinly sliced	½ cup beef broth
2 garlic cloves, minced	1 teaspoon cornstarch

Blend soy sauce and sherry in deep bowl. Add beef slices; coat well. Cover; let stand 1 hour.

Heat oil in large skillet.

Thoroughly drain beef slices on paper toweling. Sprinkle with flour. Add to hot oil; deep-fry 3 minutes. Remove meat slices with slotted spoon; drain. Set aside; keep warm.

Pour 4 tablespoons hot oil into another skillet. Discard rest of frying oil. Reheat oil. Add leeks and garlic; cook 5 minutes, stirring. Add meat slices; season with ginger, soy sauce, and anise. Pour in beef broth. Cover; simmer over very low heat 1 hour. At end of cooking time, bring to quick boil.

Blend cornstarch with small amount cold water. Add to skillet, stirring constantly until sauce is slightly thickened and bubbly. Correct seasoning if necessary. Serve immediately.

beef slices peking

tender fried round steaks

Although not as tender as other more expensive cuts of meat, round steak can be made succulent and tender in Beef Marinade. This tenderizes the steak and adds extra flavor.

1 1½-pound boneless round steak, about ½ inch thick
1 recipe Beef Marinade
2 tomatoes
Olive oil
Salt and freshly ground pepper to taste

¼ cup butter
2 tablespoons beef extract
3 teaspoons finely chopped chives
Chive Butter
Watercress (optional)

Cut steak in half; place in shallow dish. Pour marinade over steaks; refrigerate at least 24 hours, turning occasionally.

Drain steaks; set aside.

Remove stem ends from tomatoes; cut tomatoes in half. Place in shallow baking pan, cut-side-up; brush lightly with oil. Broil tomatoes 6 inches from source of heat until tender and lightly browned. Sprinkle with salt and pepper; keep warm.

Place butter in large frypan over high heat until bubbly and light brown. Place steaks in butter; cook 30 seconds. Turn; cook 30 seconds. Reduce heat to low; cook steaks 2 minutes on each side. Spoon beef extract over steaks; cook 1 minute. Steaks will be medium rare.

Place steaks on meat platter; place tomatoes around steaks.

Sprinkle 1 teaspoon chives on 4 pats Chive Butter; place 2 pats on each steak. Sprinkle remaining chives on tomatoes. Garnish with watercress if desired.

beef marinade

1 cup burgundy
½ cup olive oil
2 parsley stalks

2 sprigs tarragon
2 sprigs thyme
1 bay leaf

Combine all ingredients in small container with lid. Cover; shake to mix well.

One-eighth teaspoon dried tarragon leaves and thyme leaves can be substituted for fresh tarragon and thyme.

chive butter

½ cup unsalted butter, softened
¼ cup finely chopped chives
Salt and freshly ground pepper to taste

Place butter and chives in bowl; beat until creamy. Add salt and pepper; mix well.

Cover top of small plate with plastic wrap. Place Chive Butter on plastic wrap; shape into ½-inch-deep circle. Refrigerate until hard, then cut into circles with 1-inch canapé or cookie cutter. Remove plastic wrap from plate; push out circles from plastic-wrap side. Chive Butter can be kept in covered container in refrigerator at least 10 days.

tender fried round steaks

tomato beef

2 tablespoons cornstarch
1 tablespoon soy sauce
1 tablespoon brandy
½ pound flank steak, sliced
    ⅛ inch thick
2 tablespoons peanut oil
¼ cup chopped onion
¼ cup diagonally sliced celery
1 small green pepper, cut into 1-inch
    squares

2 tomatoes, each cut into 8 sections
¼ cup sliced water chestnuts
1 cup chicken broth, heated
1½ teaspoons catsup
½ (scant) teaspoon salt
1 teaspoon sugar
1 tablespoon cornstarch mixed with
    about 3 tablespoons cold water

Mix together cornstarch, soy sauce, and brandy. Place flank steak in mixture; marinate about 15 minutes.

Heat oil in wok or pan. Add steak; stir-fry until golden brown. Remove from pan; set aside.

Sauté onion and celery about 20 seconds. Add green pepper, tomatoes, and water chestnuts; toss several times. Add broth; cover. Let steam 1 minute; remove cover. Add beef; mix well. Cover; steam about 20 seconds. Add catsup, salt, and sugar; mix well. Thicken with cornstarch mixture. Don't let sauce get too thick.

roast beef with horseradish

Horseradish, freshly grated or bottled
Water
4 slices roast beef, each about ¹/₈ inch thick

Mix horseradish with small amount water until of spreading consistency. Spread beef with horseradish; roll up.

beef with snow peas

½ pound beef, thinly sliced

marinade

1 teaspoon cornstarch
1 teaspoon soy sauce
2 teaspoons sherry
¼ teaspoon sugar
¼ teaspoon oil

½ pound snow peas
2 teaspoons cornstarch mixed with 2
   teaspoons cold water
¹/₈ teaspoon freshly ground black
   pepper
½ teaspoon sugar
¼ teaspoon monosodium glutamate
   (MSG)
2 tablespoons oil
¼ teaspoon salt
1 teaspoon grated fresh gingerroot
½ cup chicken stock

Slice beef; set aside.
Mix marinade ingredients; marinate beef while preparing rest of ingredients.
String snow peas.
Mix together cornstarch and water. Add pepper, sugar, and MSG.
Heat skillet or wok to medium-high. Add 1 tablespoon oil, salt, and gingerroot. Add snow peas; stir. Add chicken stock; cover 10 seconds. Uncover; stir. Remove from pan.
Reheat pan; add remaining oil. When pan is hot, add beef; stir-fry only about 45 seconds, until beef is almost cooked. Add snow peas and cornstarch mixture. Stir until sauce is thickened.

beef roll-ups

Ground ginger
2 teaspoons soy sauce
8 ounces thinly sliced lean beef
½ carrot
1 scallion

1 pimiento
2 fresh mushrooms
2 tablespoons oil
2 tablespoons soy sauce
2 tablespoons mirin (sweet rice wine)

Mix small amount ginger with 2 teaspoons soy sauce. Put beef in mixture; let stand 20 minutes.

Cut carrot, scallion, pimiento, and mushrooms into thin slices.

Lay beef flat; fill with vegetables. Roll up; fasten with toothpicks.

Heat oil in skillet. Fry beef rolls, turning on all sides. Add 2 tablespoons soy sauce and mirin; turn heat higher for 1 minute. Remove toothpicks; cut roll-ups into bite-size pieces. If desired, garnish with lettuce leaves.

If you do not have mirin, you can use sherry mixed with sugar: 1 part sugar to 2 parts sherry.

beef with spinach

½ pound beef, thinly sliced

marinade

2 tablespoons rice wine or sherry
½ teaspoon salt
Freshly ground black pepper to taste
1 egg white
1 tablespoon chopped leek (onion can be substituted)

½ teaspoon grated gingerroot
1 teaspoon chili powder
1 teaspoon grated garlic
1 tablespoon cornstarch

Oil for cooking
1 tablespoon soy sauce
1 teaspoon vinegar
1¼ teaspoons sugar

1 package (10 ounces) spinach, washed, torn into bite-size pieces
Salt to taste

Cut beef into bite-size pieces.

Mix marinade ingredients; marinate beef 30 minutes.

Heat oil in skillet or wok; sauté beef over medium-high heat approximately 3 to 4 minutes. Add soy sauce, vinegar, and 1 teaspoon sugar; stir well. Remove meat mixture to serving platter.

Heat more oil if necessary; sauté spinach over high heat just until tender, 1 to 2 minutes. Add salt and remaining sugar; place on serving platter with beef.

steak tartare

½ pound fresh beef, finely chopped
1 teaspoon Worcestershire sauce
1 teaspoon cognac
1 egg yolk
Dash of Tabasco sauce
½ teaspoon paprika
¼ teaspoon salt
¼ teaspoon pepper

garnishes

Olives
Cocktail onions
Anchovy fillets with capers
Sliced gherkins
Onion, finely chopped
Crackers or thin slices of dark rye
    or pumpernickel snack bread

Place beef, Worcestershire sauce, cognac, egg yolk, Tabasco sauce, and seasonings in bowl; set in cracked ice.
Place garnishes in small bowls.
Each person spreads meat on crackers or bread; top with a garnish.

beef–rice scallop

½ cup cooked rice
½ cup chopped leftover roast beef
½ cup milk
1 egg, beaten
1 tablespoon beef drippings or margarine
1 teaspoon chopped onion
½ teaspoon salt
Few grains pepper

Mix all ingredients. Place in small greased casserole. Bake at 350°F 40 minutes.

ingredients for steak-tartare

beef in oyster sauce

1 pound lean beef, cut
  into bite-size pieces
2 tablespoons soy sauce
1 tablespoon rice wine or sherry
1 teaspoon cornstarch
Oil for cooking
1 teaspoon sugar, more or less,
  to taste
3 tablespoons oyster sauce
Cooked rice

Marinate beef in mixture of soy sauce, wine, and cornstarch 30 minutes.

Heat oil in skillet or wok to medium-high. Add beef; stir-fry until done, approximately 3 to 4 minutes. Add sugar and oyster sauce; mix well.

Serve beef with rice.

unusual beef

marinade

1 tablespoon sherry
2 tablespoons soy sauce
1 teaspoon cornstarch

½ pound lean beef, sliced, cut into
  bite-size pieces
4 tablespoons oil
3 cups potato chips
1 cup snow peas, tips broken off
Sprinkles of sherry

Blend marinade ingredients; marinate beef 15 minutes.

Heat oil to medium-high; stir-fry beef just until color changes. Add potato chips and snow peas; stir just until heated through, about 30 seconds. Sprinkle with sherry to taste. Serve immediately.

oriental hamburgers

1 pound ground beef
1 egg, beaten
¼ cup finely chopped water
    chestnuts
2 tablespoons minced onions
3 tablespoons minced mushrooms
½ teaspoon monosodium glutamate
    (MSG)
⅛ teaspoon freshly ground black
    pepper
1 tablespoon oyster sauce

Mix ground beef with remaining ingredients. Shape into 2 patties, about ¾ inch thick. Broil about 4 inches from heat, about 5 minutes. Turn; broil other side 4 to 5 minutes.

creamed dried beef

1 cup milk
½ cup white sauce
3-ounce package dried beef, torn into pieces

Stir milk into white sauce; cook and stir over low heat until thickened. Add beef; reheat. Serve immediately.

Note: If richer sauce is desired, add 2 tablespoons sour cream to creamed beef.

beef and cheese on toast

1 10-ounce can cheddar-cheese soup
¼ cup milk
1 teaspoon thick steak sauce
    (optional)
1 2-ounce jar sliced dried beef

Place soup and milk in top of double boiler; stir over boiling water until smooth. Add steak sauce.

Turn beef out onto cutting board; slice across roll three or four times. Place in strainer; pour some boiling water through meat to cut saltiness. Add drained meat to cheese-soup mixture. Place 2 slices toast on each of 2 warm plates; spoon beef–cheese mixture over them.

corned-beef patties

1 can (12 ounces) corned beef
1 cup soft bread crumbs
1 tablespoon Worcestershire sauce
1 egg
½ cup milk
1 cup flour
1 cup salad oil

Flake corned beef. Add bread crumbs and Worcestershire sauce; form into patties.

Mix egg, milk, and flour into batter.

Heat oil in skillet. Dip corned-beef patties into batter; fry in oil until golden.

beef or pork stew

1 small onion
1 medium-size carrot
1 medium-size potato
1 small stalk celery with leaves
1 cup meat broth
Sprinkle of salt
1 tablespoon flour
1 tablespoon water
⅔ cup cut-up, canned or cooked beef or pork

Cut up onion, carrot, potato, and celery.

Put broth in a pan and heat to boiling. Add cut-up fresh vegetables and salt. Cover and boil gently about 20 minutes until vegetables are tender.

Mix flour and water and slowly stir into vegetables, cooking until thickened.

Add meat and heat.

corned beef with pumpkin

½ large or 1 small pumpkin
4 onions, sliced
¼ pound butter
1 can corned beef

Peel pumpkin. Remove seeds; dice. Put pumpkin, onions, and butter into large pot; sauté until tender. Add corned beef; simmer about 5 minutes, until meat is hot. Serve this over rice.

braised lamb shanks

2 lamb shanks
2 tablespoons flour (optional)
Few grains salt
Few grains pepper
Few grains garlic salt (optional)

Coat lamb with flour. Add seasonings. Place in baking pan; cover. Bake at 325°F until tender, about 3 hours. Add water, if needed, to keep meat moistened.

Note: Lamb shanks can be cooked covered in heavy frypan or Dutch oven on top of range.

lamb shanks with creole sauce

Cook lamb as above. Pour 3 tablespoons Creole Sauce over each shank 15 minutes before end of cooking time.

creole sauce

1 tablespoon chopped onion
1 tablespoon bacon drippings
1½ teaspoons flour
1 cup cooked tomatoes
¼ cup chopped celery
¼ cup chopped green pepper
Few grains salt
Few grains pepper

Brown onion in fat. Stir in flour. Add remaining ingredients; simmer until thickened, about 20 minutes. Sauce can be stored in refrigerator a few days.

herbed lamb chops

loin lamb chops
1 teaspoon thyme
1 teaspoon oregano
1 teaspoon rosemary
3 small bay leaves, crushed
6 coriander seeds, crushed

Grated rind and juice of 1 lemon
Pinch of paprika
6 tablespoons oil
Salt and pepper
Butter

Trim excess fat from chops.

Mix herbs, lemon rind, and paprika. Rub mixture well into both sides of chops. Arrange chops on large shallow dish. Pour lemon juice and oil over chops. Season lightly with salt and pepper; set aside in cool place about 3 hours, turning occasionally.

When ready to cook, drain chops well; put on grid over hot coals. Turn once or twice while cooking, about 20 to 30 minutes.

If any dried herbs are left, a good pinch sprinkled over hot coals just before you remove chops will give a delicious aroma and improve the flavor.

Serve chops with pat of butter on each and plain tossed salad.

herbed lamb chops

mixed grill

2 lamb loin or rib chops, cut
    ¾ to 1 inch thick
2 slices liver, cut in half (optional);
    chicken livers can be used
Cooking oil
2 sausages (your choice)
4 chunks green pepper, 1-inch square
4 cherry tomatoes
3 large mushroom caps

Brush chops and livers with oil.

On skewer place 1 sausage half, then ½ liver slice, piece of green pepper, 1 lamb chop, second piece of green pepper, another liver half, and another sausage. Repeat until all are used. Grill 3 to 4 inches from source of heat about 20 minutes or until desired degree of doneness, turning once.

kidney stew

4 veal kidneys
3 bay leaves
1 carrot, thinly sliced
2 whole cloves
$^1/_8$ teaspoon cayenne pepper
½ lemon
$^1/_8$ teaspoon mace
$^1/_8$ teaspoon nutmeg

Parboil and drain kidneys about 4 times or until water stays clear. Save half of last water. Cool and thinly slice kidneys, cutting away membrane. Add to saved water with remaining ingredients, using both juice and rind of lemon. Simmer until carrot is tender. Thicken to consistency of cream.

Serve stew hot on slices of rye bread.

veal parmesan

2 veal cutlets
Italian bread crumbs or seasoned
bread crumbs mixed with
Parmesan cheese
1 egg, beaten with a little water
Oil for frying
2 slices mozzarella cheese
1 can Arturo or tomato sauce

Roll veal in bread crumbs. Dip in egg; roll in crumbs again. Refrigerate several hours.

Brown cutlets in oil on both sides in skillet. Place in oven dish; top with cheese and sauce. Bake at 350°F 30 minutes.

veal parmesan

ham barbecue

1 fully cooked smoked ham slice,
    cut ¾ to 1 inch thick
¾ cup catsup
1 tablespoon lemon juice

1½ tablespoons brown sugar
1 tablespoon dijon-style mustard
1 tablespoon Worcestershire sauce
1 teaspoon chili powder

Place ham in baking dish.

Combine remaining ingredients. Brush both sides of meat liberally with sauce; let stand 1 hour.

Place ham on grill 3 to 5 inches from low to medium coals; cook 5 to 6 minutes per side, turning once and brushing with sauce.

ham–potato casserole

1 cup mashed potato
⅔ cup chopped cooked smoked ham
2 teaspoons finely chopped onion
2 teaspoons butter or margarine
¼ cup shredded cheese

Mix potato and ham.

Cook onion in butter until clear but not brown. Add onion to potato mixture. Place mixture in small casserole; top with cheese. Bake at 375°F until top begins to brown and cheese is melted, about 25 minutes.

Note: Dehydrated mashed potatoes can be used. Prepare potatoes according to package directions.

cranberry-glazed pork chops

2 pork chops, 1 inch thick
1 small clove garlic, mashed
Salt and pepper
1 tablespoon butter or margarine
½ cup apple juice
⅓ cup jellied cranberry sauce
⅓ cup applesauce
Dash of ground cloves

Rub chops with garlic; sprinkle with salt and pepper.

Heat butter in skillet; brown chops well on both sides. Add apple juice; cover tightly. Simmer 1 hour or until pork is fork-tender.

Drain pan juices into a bowl; stir in cranberry sauce and applesauce. Beat until well blended. Stir in cloves. Spoon mixture over chops. Place chops under broiler; broil until mixture is bubbly.

pork and turnips

2 lean pork chops
1 tablespoon shortening
4 small young turnips, sliced
½ medium-size onion, sliced
10½-ounce can condensed cream of
    mushroom soup
⅓ cup milk
Few grains salt
Few grains pepper

Brown chops in fat.

Place layer of turnip slices in baking pan. Place chops over turnips; top with layer of sliced onion.

Combine soup, milk, and seasonings; pour over onion. Bake at 350°F until chops are tender, about 1 hour.

barbecued pork chops

pork chops

2 lean pork chops, 1-inch thick
1 teaspoon flour
Few grains salt
Few grains pepper
1 tablespoon shortening

barbecue sauce

¼ cup tomato paste
1⅓ tablespoons vinegar
2 tablespoons brown sugar
¼ teaspoon allspice
¼ teaspoon cloves

Coat chops with flour mixed with seasonings. Brown chops in fat. Place in baking pan or casserole.

Mix sauce ingredients; cook over low heat 2 minutes.

Pour sauce over chops. Bake, uncovered, at 350°F until chops are tender, about 1 hour.

Note: Chops can be cooked on top of range.

pork-chop skillet dinner

1 tablespoon cooking oil
Salt and pepper to taste
2 large thick pork chops
2 large potatoes, peeled, sliced
1 8-ounce can tiny peas
1 can cream of mushroom soup

Heat oil in skillet.

Salt and pepper chops on both sides; brown in oil, turning once. Push chops to back of skillet. Add potatoes; sprinkle with a little salt and pepper. Fry, turning, until potatoes are lightly browned. Rearrange chops so they continue to cook at one side of skillet. Place chops over potatoes. Mix peas, juice and all, with soup; pour over all. Cover; bake at 350°F about 25 minutes or until meat is tender.

skewered japanese pork

1 pound pork, cut into bite-size
    pieces, ½ inch thick
1 small eggplant, cut into bite-size
    cubes
4 or 5 scallions, cut into 1½-inch
    lengths
2 green peppers, cut into chunks
Flour for dredging
Oil for frying
Soy sauce (optional)

Skewer pork, eggplant, scallions, and peppers on skewers. Dredge in flour; fry in oil about 4 minutes or until browned. Remove from oil; brush with soy sauce.

Serve pork with rice.

chinese pork with peas

12 ounces lean pork

marinade

2 tablespoons soy sauce
2 teaspoons sherry
$\frac{1}{8}$ teaspoon monosodium glutamate
  (MSG)
1 egg white
1 teaspoon cornstarch
Salt
White pepper

4 ounces frozen peas
8 tablespoons oil
$\frac{1}{2}$ cup hot beef broth
Salt
Sugar
1 leek, cut into julienne strips
1 clove garlic, minced
1 4-ounce can sliced mushrooms
1 4-ounce can bamboo shoots
1 preserved ginger, sliced
1 tablespoon sherry
1 tablespoon cornstarch
2 teaspoons soy sauce
2 tablespoons oyster sauce
White pepper
Pinch of powdered ginger

Cut meat crosswise into thin strips.
Prepare marinade. Combine and blend soy sauce, sherry, MSG, egg white, and cornstarch. Season to taste with salt and white pepper.
Pour marinade over pork; cover. Let marinate 30 minutes.
Meanwhile thaw peas.
Heat 2 tablespoons oil in small saucepan. Add peas; pour in beef broth. Season to taste with salt and sugar; cook 5 minutes. Drain peas, reserving cooking liquid; keep warm.
Heat 3 tablespoons oil in large saucepan. Add leek, garlic, mushrooms, bamboo shoots, and ginger; cook 5 minutes, stirring constantly. Set aside; keep warm.
Heat rest of oil in skillet. Add meat and marinade; cook 3 minutes or until meat is browned, stirring occasionally. Add meat and peas to large saucepan with vegetables. Pour in sherry and reserved cooking liquid; bring to boil.
Blend cornstarch with soy and oyster sauces; stir until slightly thickened and bubbly. Season to taste with salt, pepper, ginger, and sugar. Serve immediately.

chinese pork with peas

sausage and applesauce

½ pound sausages
3 tomatoes, halved
3 medium potatoes
2 tablespoons butter
⅝ cup applesauce

Pinch of curry powder
1 teaspoon lemon juice
Salt and pepper
Chopped parsley

Fry sausages gently until brown all over and cooked thoroughly. Add tomatoes; cook gently.

Meanwhile boil potatoes. Drain; mash well. Add butter, heated applesauce, curry powder, lemon juice, and seasoning; mix well.

Spoon or pipe onto warm serving dish. Arrange sausages and tomatoes on top; decorate with parsley.

Alternatively, omit tomatoes, and instead of adding applesauce to potatoes, use plain mashed potatoes and add grilled apple slices to the dish as garnish.

chinese spareribs

barbecued spareribs

6 tablespoons soy sauce
6 tablespoons water
2 tablespoons dry sherry
2 tablespoons lemon juice
2 cloves garlic, minced
3 pounds center-cut spareribs, cut and trimmed
3 to 4 tablespoons honey

Combine soy sauce, water, sherry, lemon juice, and garlic. Pour over ribs; marinate 2 to 3 hours. Turn ribs in sauce occasionally.

Preheat oven to 350°F.

Place ribs side by side in large deep roasting pan. Cover with marinating sauce; dribble with honey. Roast about 1½ hours or until done, turning frequently. (A slight amount of water may have to be added during roasting.)

chinese spareribs

1½ pounds pork spareribs
¾ cup beef bouillon
¼ cup brown sugar
2 tablespoons soy sauce
¼ teaspoon garlic powder

Separate pork into single ribs. Marinate several hours in other ingredients. Baste while baking in 9 × 13-inch pan. Bake 1 hour and 45 minutes at 350°F.

desserts

Top off your meal with more than just a pre-packaged cupcake or a bakery bought pie. Try the dessert delights included here and be a creative cook in your own home.

fruit bowl

1 can mandarin oranges, drained
1 apple, peeled, sliced
1 banana, sliced, sprinkled with lime
    or lemon juice
6 dates, cut in half
$^1/_8$ cup walnut chips

   Place oranges in glass bowl. Combine with apple, banana, and dates. Sprinkle with walnut chips.

fruit bowl

126

fried bananas

4 to 6 ripe bananas
½ cup butter
Sugar
½ teaspoon cinnamon
1 tablespoon lemon juice

Slice bananas into bite-size pieces.

Melt butter in skillet; add bananas. Fry few minutes; sprinkle with sugar mixed with cinnamon. Squeeze lemon juice on top.

Serve bananas with plain cake or ice cream.

orange bananas

2 ripe bananas
Whipped cream
Orange honey to taste
Freshly shredded orange rind

Peel and halve bananas crosswise. Heat in a little butter in skillet. Top with whipped cream sweetened with orange honey; sprinkle with orange rind.

cream-topped grapes

30 large green grapes
4 ounces whipped cream cheese
2 tablespoons sour cream
Maple sugar to taste

Halve and seed grapes; pile into sherbet glasses. Top each with whipped cream cheese fluffed up with sour cream; add sprinkling of maple sugar; or, pass chesse mixture and maple sugar separately.

rum grapefruit

1 seedless grapefruit
2 tablespoons brown sugar
2 tablespoons rum

Halve grapefruit; cut around sections to loosen them. With kitchen scissors clip out center membrane from each half to make small cavity for juices to run into. Spread each half with 1 tablespoon brown sugar; sprinkle each with 1 tablespoon rum. Broil about 4 inches from high heat until hot. Serve at once.

orange-cup dessert

A very pretty and refreshing dessert.

orange-cup dessert

2 oranges with unblemished skin
Fruit such as:
    Pineapple
    Orange sections
    Grapefruit sections
    Bananas
    Maraschino cherries
    Walnuts

Cut slice from top of each orange so insides can be scooped out.
Combine any of above fruits, or others of your choice; spoon into orange shells. Refrigerate until serving time.
The same thing can be done with grapefruit or bananas, as pictured. If desired, a small amount of your favorite liqueur can be added to the fruit.

orange and pineapple compote

1 small can mandarin oranges in light syrup
1 can crushed pineapple in own juice

Mix ingredients in bowl; chill. Serve in brandy snifters.

oranges in wine

2 or 3 oranges
Dry red wine
Sugar to taste

Cut peel from each orange so no white membrane remains. (Use small sharp knife; cut from top to bottom in strips, or round and round in spiral fashion.) Slice oranges fairly thin.

Sweeten wine by stirring in sugar. Add oranges. Give flavors time to blend. Serve chilled.

pear treat

A nice treat to serve with a glass of sherry wine.

1 fresh California Bartlett pear
3 tablespoons cream cheese,
    softened
1 tablespoon blue cheese, softened
1 tablespoon almonds, chopped
Candied ginger to taste

Cut pear in half; remove core.

Blend cheeses; stir in amonds and ginger. Fill pear halves with cheese mixture; garnish with almonds.

pear sundae

A quickie dessert can be very pretty, too.

1 fresh Bartlett pear
Vanilla ice cream
Hot fudge sauce

Cut pear in half. Place halves in 2 dessert dishes. Fill hollows with ice cream. Top with sauce.

easy festive ice cream

Shredded coconut
Ice cream of your choice
Tia Maria coffee or Peter Herring cherry liqueur

Toast shredded coconut in very low oven 5 minutes. Sprinkle over ice cream. Top with liqueur.

fresh lemon ice cream

2 cups half-and-half or heavy cream
1 cup sugar
1 to 2 tablespoons freshly grated
    lemon peel
⅓ cup fresh-squeezed lemon juice

Stir together cream and sugar in large bowl until sugar is thoroughly dissolved. Mix in lemon peel and juice. Pour into ice-cube tray, 8-inch-square pan, or directly into sherbet dishes. Freeze several hours, until firm.

chocolate–orange mousse

½ teaspoon grated orange rind
2 tablespoons packed light-brown
    sugar
1 egg yolk
1 egg
3 squares (3 ounces) semisweet
    chocolate, melted, cooled
1½ tablespoons orange juice
½ cup heavy cream

Combine rind, sugar, egg yolk, and egg in a blender; whirl until light and foamy. Add chocolate, orange juice, and cream; whirl until well blended. Pour into 2 dessert dishes; chill about 1 hour, until set.

yogurt fruit sundaes

2 scoops (⅔ cup) vanilla frozen
    yogurt
8 or 10 ripe strawberries, sliced
4 tablespoons undiluted defrosted
    orange-juice concentrate

Place 1 scoop yogurt in each of 2 dessert dishes. Surround each with berries; drizzle orange juice on top.

italian pudding

⅝ cup cake crumbs
⅝ cup bread crumbs
6 macaroons, pounded
3 tablespoons finely chopped
    candied peel
1½ tablespoons raisins
2 tablespoons shredded pistachio
    nuts
1 tablespoon rum or brandy
2 eggs

Put cake and bread crumbs, macaroons, peel, raisins, and nuts into bowl.
Beat together brandy and eggs; stir into crumb mixture. Turn into well-greased mold. Steam gently 1 to 1¼ hours. Serve with Custard Sauce.

custard sauce

2 teaspoons sugar
2 egg yolks or 1 whole egg
1¼ cups milk
Flavoring

Mix together sugar and egg yolks.
Warm milk until about lukewarm, preferably in top of double boiler. Stir milk into egg. Return everything to rinsed pan; cook over low heat until egg thickens without boiling, or the egg will curdle. At once pour out of pan into bowl or sauce boat. Flavor; add extra sweetening if desired. If custard should curdle, beat it vigorously just before serving.

beverages

You may not find plain coffee or tea included here, but you're sure to enjoy a Tropical Twist if you want a non-alcoholic cooler. Or complete your gourmet delight for two with Irish Coffee — a drink which will warm up any cold feet on a long winter's night. And here's to happy cooking and your very good health.

cucumber cooler

1 cup chilled unsweetened pineapple
     juice
1 cup peeled, seeded cucumber
     chunks
½ cup watercress
2 sprigs parsley
½ cup finely crushed ice

Place all in blender; blend until smooth.

grape frost

Frothy and refreshing.

1 cup grape juice
1 cup plain yogurt
4 or 5 ice cubes

Place all ingredients in blender; blend until smooth. Serve at once.

tropical twist

1½ cups chilled unsweetened
     pineapple juice
1 ripe banana
2 teaspoons honey
Juice of ½ lime
½ cup finely crushed ice

Place all in blender; blend until smooth.

strawberry or blueberry shake

1 cup plain yogurt
½ to ¾ cup fresh strawberries or
    blueberries
1 to 2 tablespoons honey
4 ice cubes

Combine all ingredients in blender; blend until smooth. Enjoy at once.

strawberry shake

irish coffee

2 heaping teaspoons instant coffee
    powder
2 full teaspoons sugar
2 jiggers Irish whiskey
2 cups boiling water
Whipped cream

Divide coffee, sugar, and whiskey between 2 cups; mix well. Add boiling water until almost full. Spoon whipped cream on top in mounds. Serve immediately.

lemon cocktail

lemon cocktail

Juice of 2 lemons
Juice of 1 orange
2 teaspoons honey
4 jiggers sherry
6 ice cubes
2 lemon slices
2 orange slices
4 maraschino cherries

Shake juices, honey, and sherry in cocktail shaker. Crush ice cubes; place in 2 tall glasses. Pour lemon cocktail over ice. Peel lemon and orange slices. Cut into small pieces; add to drinks. Garnish with cherries.

135

piña colada

1 cup coconut juice (available
   canned)
1 cup pineapple juice
4 to 6 tablespoons honey or sugar
8 to 10 ice cubes
½ cup rum

Combine all ingredients in blender jar; blend until smooth. Serve at once in tall glasses.

creme de menthe pickup

1 tablespoon grenadine
Sugar
½ cup cold milk
½ cup plain yogurt
¼ cup creme de menthe
2 tablespoons cointreau

Pour grenadine into small, shallow bowl.
Place sugar in second dish.
Dip rims of glasses in grenadine, then in sugar.
Blend milk, yogurt, creme de menthe, and cointreau in a blender until smooth.
Pour into prepared glasses. Serve immediately.

creme de menthe pickup

chocolate brandy

2 scoops chocolate ice cream
1 cup plain yogurt
2 tablespoons brandy
Whipped cream (garnish)
Cocoa (garnish)

Place ice cream, yogurt, and brandy in blender; blend until smooth. Pour into glasses. Garnish with whipped cream and pinch of cocoa.

chocolate brandy

menus

The recipes listed below and on the following pages are included in this book.

luncheons

Luncheons for two can be much more interesting than an everyday sandwich, salad or soup.

Crab-Meat Salad
Fresh Asparagus
Yogurt Fruit Sundaes

Stuffed Pineapple
Tomato and Herb Salad
Easy Festive Ice Cream

Chicken Club Sandwich
Orange Bananas

Oyster Bisque
Grapefruit Mold

Tuna Salad
Green-Pepper Sauté

Greek-Goddess Salad
Orange and Pineapple Compote

light suppers

Omelets are so quick and easy to prepare that they are an excellent choice as part of a couple's light supper.

Zucchini Omelet
Fruit Salad
Fresh Lemon Ice Cream

Chicken-Liver Omelet
Quick-and-Easy Cucumber Salad
Oranges in Wine

Mushroom Omelet
Spinach Salad
Cream-Topped Grapes

dinners

These full-course dinners illustrate the elegance of cooking for two.

Pineapple Duck
Beet Salad
Delicious Spinach
Italian Pudding

Braised Lamb Shanks
Carrot Pennies
Orange-Cup Dessert

Egg Foo Yong
Chinese Pork with Peas
Tomato and Herb Salad
Rum Grapefruit

Potato Soup
Flounder Stuffed with Crab
Green Beans Italian
Chocolate-Orange Mousse

Tomato Fondue with Cocktail Frankfurters
Broiled Spring Chicken
Orange and Onion Salad
Breaded Fried Eggplant Sticks
Easy Festive Ice Cream

Oyster Bisque
Veal Parmesan
Marinated Vegetables
Pear Sundaes

Clams Casino
Avocado Salad Vinaigrette
Spaghetti with Génoise Sauce
Fresh Lemon Ice Cream

index